2⁰⁰

New Hungers for Old: One-Hundred Years of Italian-American Poetry

New Hungers for Old:
One-Hundred Years of Italian-American Poetry

Edited by Dennis Barone

Star Cloud Press
Scottsdale, Arizona

New Hungers for Old:
One-Hundred Years of
Italian-American Poetry

Cover art: Joseph Stella, *Brooklyn Bridge*
Yale University Art Gallery,
Gift of Collection Société Anonyme

Cover design: Trish Hadley

Published by

~Star Cloud Press®~
6137 East Mescal Street
Scottsdale, Arizona 85254-5418

ISBN:

978-1-932842-52-4 — $ 19.95

Library of Congress Control Number: 2011931274

Printed in the United States of America

Table of Contents

Preface

Dennis Barone

In 2009 James Finnegan and I co-edited the University of Iowa Press anthology *Visiting Wallace: Poems Inspired by the Life and Work of Wallace Stevens.* How does one get from Stevens to Italian Americans? Stevens once wrote to his friend Thomas McGreevy: "Rome is not ordinarily on the itinerary of my imagination." And yet Italy and things Italian often appear prominent in this Francophile's exquisite poetry. Twelve poets make an appearance in both *Visiting Wallace* and *New Hungers from Old.*

In 2008 at the Modern Language Association Convention in San Francisco I organized a session on Italian American Literary Innovation. The three excellent papers delivered considered the prose of Pietro di Donato, Gilbert Sorrentino, and Carole Maso. All of the subjects are clearly poetic in their prose style, but that isn't quite to say poetry. (Of course, Sorrentino was a brilliant poet and so too is Maso and their work has been included herein.) More important to the purpose here of introducing an ethnic-identity based anthology is this: when the session finished and we had some minutes for discussion I wondered and had occasion to ask the speakers and audience, although Italian American ethnicity connects these three writers what in the writing itself connects them?

Josephine Gattuso Hendin replied with a most amazing answer *ex tempore*. She claimed the following connects di Donato, Sorrentino, and Maso. And I add that this formulation may be equally true for the one-hundred-poets in the present volume. Jo Hendin said the common core characteristics are an attack on sexual convention, an urge to linguistic impulse and adventure, an emphasis on musicality and emotion, and—to return to the sexual—an intense connection with sexuality as the key element in a rebellion against restrictions embodied in family, church, and narrative plot itself (might I say poetic form itself?).

The poems in *New Hungers for Old* do indeed have intense emotionality and rich musicality or undertake an adventure in form that attacks convention, poetic and otherwise. Maso's poem comes from a book of erotica. And I have tried to be broadly representative within the confines set by one ethnic identity. Yes, there are poems of food, faith, and family, but there are also ones of the worker's plight and ones where the words themselves (not an external and explicit reference outside of the poem) do the poem's work. The oldest poem, Arturo Giovannetti's "The Bum" is one hundred years old and the most recent is very recent, indeed: perhaps, from just yesterday or the day before. This volume that presents one-hundred years of poetry by immigrants, their children, grandchildren, and great grandchildren, includes realist, modernist, and postmodernist poets; formalists and non-traditionalists; worker-poets and doctor-poets. One ethnicity does not necessary mean a precise uniformity and a lack of variety. I have included poets from some of the main Italian American presses such as Bordighera Press and Guernica Editions as well as poets from university and large commercial presses.

One of the volume's contributors, Tony Quagliano, opened a brief essay he wrote on ethnic identity with the claim that "ethnicity is the last refuge of scroundrels [...]." His satire poked fun at ethnicity in the manner of so many coffee table picture books or pride-in-the-ancestors television documentaries. I don't think there's a single poem herein that celebrates *italianità* in that simplistic manner.

These poems in their variety of forms address matters of ethnic shame perhaps more often than ones of pride. There are expressions of anger aplenty, but also ones of humor. The title comes from a line in Emanuel Carnevali's well-known poem "The Return" and some of the poems in this anthology address returning to the ancestral country or, more specifically, town. Others speak of the arrival of immigrants to America. Carnevali's poem, "Italian Farmer," he once told Ezra Pound he thought his best. And yes these poets may be Italian or Italian American, but they are also poets and not all the poems directly address things Italian-American. As Gilbert Sorrentino long ago suggested, a poet may "come in from a different angle" (or would some like that to be "angel"?).

The poems included also come from different times in a poet's career. One might assume that a poet writes about identity early (finding out) or late (summarizing a life) in a career, but many of the poems are from mid-point and some have nothing to do with an explicit identity at all and express *italianità* in some other way altogether, a manner that awaits your discovery and pleasure as you read.

I thank Kathleen Kelley, librarian extraordinaire, for securing many books via interlibrary loan, I thank Lew Turco for assistance and advice, I thank Patricia Mango Senich for helping me prepare the manuscript, and I thank two good friends in poetry James Finnegan and Peter Covino.

Introduction

Mary Caponegro

I'm not sure what I can add to Dennis Barone's fine preface, except to say how moved I was by reading this sequence of poems: moved by the consistent beauty of the lines and images and narratives, moved by the fact that all the authors were of Italian heritage, an ethnic group which has not enjoyed the reputation of a strong contemporary literary legacy. Many anthologies, when all is said and done, feel haphazard, circumstantial, forced. Not this one. Perhaps the most remarkable thing is the way one poem seems to inform the next, even if unconsciously — that a poem explicitly referencing an ancestral home might seem to generate another poem whose relation to that ancestral home is oblique or even non-existent. In a time when American poetry can seem irreconcilably divided into camps, these poems speak to each other outside the divide, in a zone of dignity, resourcefulness and integrity, and in a solidarity that feels organic.

The anthology comfortably occupies numerous rhetorical registers, and I suspect it serves several purposes. If you happen to be Italian-American, it will give you something to connect to through a shared heritage and familiar images, and the collective formal mastery of these poets will elicit considerable pride. If you don't happen to be Italian-American, it will give you a coherent but never reductive sense of what constitutes Italian-American identity. If you're tired of the aforementioned poetry wars, this anthology will rescue you from the ideological divide, since here formal innovation and traditionalism stand side by side, enriching the mixture.

These poems move from gravitas to deadpan, from elegiac to anarchic, from Ciardi and Galasssi, for example, to Guida, whose risqué refutation of roots is a gesture of liberation and rebellion, reminding us of the place of blasphemy and parody in Italian culture. Covino's poem of coming out to his conservative Italian family on Easter Sunday similarly embraces contradiction. Religion undergoes numerous permutations as Skoyles grapples with both a disappearing priest and a disappearing God. And Barbarese reconfigures Eucharist as loot — when a harshly treated immigrant tries to make a statement to the society that presses upon him.

How can I articulate just what it is that makes these poems so evocative? Form and content seem so beautifully married in each, and the ethnic subject matter we find so often sentimentalized or stereotyped is treated here with sophistication and depth.

The figure of the immigrant moves hauntingly through a number of these poems, as one might expect. So does poverty and hardship and the fruit of the land. So does the church and its rituals. Language itself animates these poems: a preoccupation with words, with proper nouns, with names (as in Anania and Tufariello), the tension between an ancestral tongue and a modern, more practical one.

The geography that animates these poems will not surprise you though it will entrance you, regardless of whether it takes the form of places lived in, memorized or dreamt. You will visit Brooklyn (courtesy of Diane di Prima and Donna Masini), the Bronx, Little Italy — and of course there is the boot itself, explored mostly from Rome through Sicily (Ciardi's roots near Vesuvius, for instance). The verdant expanse of the Gianicolo figures in Galassi's poem, which offers us an elegant verbal journey through the Doria Pamphili Park, and Kara Candito's "Postcard" moves us through the architectural splendor of the ancient city, with a particular emotional intensity. Many regions of Italy, often more humble ones, are featured in these pages.

The standard cliché which represents Italian life consisting of a surfeit of maternal nurture along with a surfeit of delectable food is debunked as Dorothy Barresi introduces us to a boy (her father) who was hauled off to an orphanage for leaving squash uneaten on his plate, and Tambellini remembers the emergency wartime nutrition of the scorned-as-weed dandelion. Perhaps at the root of it all, Carnevali's farmer works the land with all its harshness. More sobering still, Mobilio's "Pilgrims" give us an existential snapshot of a dreamlike journey from nothing to even less. Polite presents the bracingly un-romanticized view that has "learned to leave well enough alone" — a resignation that is not so much bitter as measured.

Some of these poems serve up politics from an Italian-American perspective. Tusiani's "Bicentennial" articulates the immigrant's bifurcation. And Tammaro's scathing "Richard M. Nixon: My Italian Problem" tackles more insidious contradictions. These and other socially directed poems resonate majestically with the Whitmanesque strains of Ferlinghetti, ever relevant.

Papaleo, in "History Lessons for Friday," sweeps us forward, extrapolating from Italian immigration to the bigotries endured by other ethnic groups who modify themselves accordingly to be assimilated and accepted. Appellations such as "Pop the Wop" and "Tony the Dago" remind us of the bigotry that served to color many of the upbringings referenced here. (Such is the incisiveness of ethnic humor in this anthology that we can eavesdrop in Anania's poem on an Italian-American child innocently calling an adult Mrs. Tony the Dago!)

The war is often remembered in these pages, and in doing so, Diana Festa invokes Fellini's *La Dolce Vita*, though we may through the uncompromising clarity of these poems, be inclined to resurrect the neorealist images of De Sica or Rossellini.

Michael Palmer, Leslie Scalapino, and others, inhabit a more abstract, perhaps more multivalent realm, with a more experimental textual representation, yet seem to flow quite naturally from their more traditionalist kin, as does Ceravolo in his hypnotic simplicity. Scalapino's abstracted event floats tantalizingly over the more concrete events that populate the poems of other poets — tragic or somber events, such as the suicide of a woman who resembled the woman on a Medaglia D'Oro coffee can, or a world war, or a funeral, or a religious procession on Good Friday.

Memory is a sensually powerful force throughout these poems: memory of an ancestral past, of another land, of war, of starting over, of grandparents and parents, of lovers, of lost languages and compromised allegiances. Perhaps memory is all the more intense in these poems, since by their very inclusion they are connected to a history that harkens back to antiquity. One feels the yearning to connect a new world to an old one, whether one wishes to caress that world, efface it, complicate it or immortalize it.

After Barone has moved us masterfully through a hundred years, we might allow Ciardi's words to sum it up most eloquently: "We sit in whatever century we are left in."

Kim Addonizio

GENERATIONS

Somewhere a shop of hanging meats,
shop of stink and blood, block and cleaver;

somewhere an immigrant, grandfather, stranger
with my last name. That man

untying his apron in 1910, scrubbing off
the pale fat, going home past brownstones

and churches, past vendors, streetcars, arias,
past the clatter of supper dishes, going home

to his new son, my father—
What is he to me, butcher with sausage fingers,

old Italian leaning over a child somewhere
in New York City, somewhere alive, what is he

that I go back to look for him, years after his death
and my father's death, knowing only

a name, a few scraps my father fed me?
My father who shortened that name, who hacked off

three lovely syllables, who raised American children.
What is the past to me

that I have to go back, pronouncing that word
in the silence of a cemetery, what is this stone

coming apart in my hands like bread, name
I eat and expel? Somewhere the smell of figs

and brine, strung garlic, rosemary and olives;
somewhere that place. Somewhere a boat

rocking, crossing over, entering the harbor. I wait
on the dock, one face in a crowd of faces.

Families disembark and stream toward the city,
and though I walk among them for hours,

hungry, haunting the streets,
I can't tell which of them is mine.

Somewhere a steak is wrapped in thick paper,
somewhere my grandmother is laid in the earth,

and my young father shines shoes on a corner,
turning his back to the Old World, forgetting.

I walk the night city, looking up at lit windows,
and there is no table set for me, nowhere

I can go to be filled. This is the city
of grandparents, immigrants, arrivals,

where I've come too late with my name,
an empty plate. This is the place.

Joe Amato

Hotel

But I hasten to add
that America, its landscape of Super
8's or some aspect of it
as ~~once~~ I once knew it
and as I am coming to know it a-
new, at once courtesy of
( )
and
(heartbreak
hotel of course)
will play a key role here
and not merely as the prevailing planetary source
of neoliberal possibility and
crazy privatized woe.

My wife Kass
(I have a wife
named Kass
who fancies herself something of an economist
of sorts
and a wife)
interjects, accordingly, over the din
of bad classic rock
I subject myself to daily
to atone for the lip
service I pay

to the simpler life
I once enjoyed ~~once~~:

"Will the mass luxury market create good jobs
for the many
as some are claiming
it will do, and will it do
so without meanwhile
for instance
destroying the planet?"
(I am paraphrasing
reception fuzzy)

We both sip our Starbucks decaf house blend
(she takes Splenda)
our brows deeply furrowed
as we brainstorm, develop
a plan to enter

the fourth quintile, a place
we, or at least I
imagine
of duty-free collaboration
and superb cheeses.

(She really does.)

Michael Anania

OMAHA APPENDICES: IV

In the *Omaha City Directory*
for 1914 my great-grandfather
is listed at 2618 Rees Street
as "Angelo Anannea, laborer,"
his last name, only that one time, misspelled;
on the same page his sons are listed
at their own addresses as Dominic
and Michael Anania. It is hard
to know whether the old man, by then
already sixty-three, gave them the wrong
spelling in order to preserve the sound
of his name, which in Italian rhymes
with Pangea or Judea and not as
I pronounce it in English rhyming with
Jeremiah or if, which is more likely,
the census-taker wrote it out in what
he thought was phonetic English,
Anannea for Anania then, which may
in turn be the reason the family
in Omaha, only, adopted
the long i-sound to pronounce its name,
trading one loss for another, which is
a step you take away from yourself,
part of becoming, in time, American.
So Gigliotti became Gigliotti,
pronounced Gillottee or Gillot pronounced

Gillat or Gellati pronounced Gellati
and Pane, the two syllable word for bread,
became the one syllable Pane, as in Payne
and Peri became Perry, Michele
Michael, then Mike, Domenico Dominic
eventually Donny, Giovanna
Jenny, Giuseppe Joseph, then Joe,
Giuseppina Josie, Raffaele
Ralph, Pietro Pete, Francesco Frank.
No one complained, really; what loss
there was came so easily. Italian first
names were reserved for evening whispers,
for consolations and novenas.
Sometime in the thirties a distant cousin,
named Antonio Georgioni, went
to court and changed his name officially
to Anthony George; Tony George was what
he had in mind, a real American name,
but in the neighborhood from then on
he was called "Tony the Dago,"
a comic reproach so uniformly
applied that until I was fifteen or so
it was the only name I knew for him.
Once, confounded, but trying to be polite,
I called his wife Mrs. Tony the Dago.
She scowled at me and told my father
that he had better teach me some manners.
Sometime in the forties, though Italy
remained Italy, the adjective became
eye-talian, not Italian or Italiano,
so you went to the store for eye-talian

bread or eye-talian canned tomatoes
and spoke, whenever you spoke it, eye-talian,
an insult having become the word
in American for everything you cherished.

Christopher Arigo

Archived imperatives I

(A) I will show you where to stand
but the rooms are oblivious—the walls
the chair gently rocking itself
—to camouflage / *to disguise* / to hide among
sunrises—this is when we depart or
concede to *terra firma* duped by gravity or
baited by the seductive tuck of a bed
—the startling realness of some firm ground
when you expel one breath
in the name of exchange
withhold the other
in a game called survival
and do not share the spasms
that interfere with sleep

(B) Euphemize *mystery as terra incognita*
—an afflicted region / a stigmatized tract of shoulder
of shadow defining muscle
—a tract of land and water
tattooed on your stomach: *corpus incognito*
—as you pace the house vertical blinds cast striae
and accentuate your body's contours
—as you dictate your will indwelling
on the inception of light-ribbons
into every corner—we attempt momentary forays
into confusion to refute

what precedes future / what hinders us
what is hidden in the archives

(C)When walls sweat and buckle and
breathe / when air crackles with
staticky danger / when branch-heaps shelter rabbits
who leave misleading trails in widening spirals
—after a phoenix egg is conflagration and
the television's vertical shift
means more than it should
and when trumpet vines finally overwhelm
the awnings-then intestate but smiling
we can end and begin here

Anny Ballardini

They came from the same place

They came from the same place
listed first under Austria
then under Italy
a small village in the north
snow in winter _ summers short
static-free
leaving
feverishly drawn
devouring their cheeks
the vast land
their other mother
barely in their teens
*
jobs on offer
a distant cousin, a father, someone
there with an address
150 dollars in *his* pocket
hair: natural / no particular signs / tall, healthy
with their trades / their resolve / their virtues in their hands
days & days the ocean cutting the sky
the sky the ocean

They came with La Gascogne / Olympic _ with Sofia Hohenberg
_ La Provence _ Dante Alighieri / Conte Verde _ City of Paris
– Saint Louis _ France _ Kaiser Franz Joseph / renamed President
Wilson _ with
Finland

superb ships
grotesque iron whales
clanging whirring hooting
distancing/approaching
gliding nearer/spacing out
mapping through
they
talking in the air
to the winds
to the water /
electricity their dreams
electric
lights

projected ahead fragments of future glittering water in
bouncing back sparks unfenced by swishing swirls whirls
from the mirroring mosaics shining on fluid arabesques waves soothing
myriads of suns of crushing waves lulling
breaking echoing from the harsh call emerald
against of gulls the thumps loving
the waves' white crests of jumping dolphins their Mermaids' song

from that future
I glimpse to meet you
my great- and grand-/Fathers, father
my face, left hand, recomposing my sternum
sitting_more comfortably_inside myself
with a small rose clip

J. T. Barbarese

Our Fathers

stole useless supplies
from Westinghouse and Bruders,
worked third shift, punched in and out,
felt shiftless, like intruders,

so walked off with expensive tools,
rivet guns, dies, and gauges
fine enough for tolerances
thinner than these pages,

built boxes for the tools they stole,
milled from purloined steel
they squirreled away when the shifts changed.
They stole things just to steal,

crazy stuff — graphite, vises, bar steel,
pulley wheels, mounts and rings,
sanders, calipers, bolts, even rope
to lash down everything

we'd tie in our flight from nuclear death
to the roofs of the used cars
we helped them wax on Sundays
when the corner shot-and-a-beer bars

they closed the night before were dark
and we were off at mass.
They preached the American gospel
of hard work means success

and the immigrant religion
whose eucharist was loot.
Life itself was stolen goods.
They're buried in stolen suits.

Dennis Barone

Map

A song of bridges

And then a silence

At one time

There were no stones

Oak rippled water

And an oar-less boat

At night: darkness

As expected; then morning

A wing that beats

The silence back

Dorothy Barresi

My Anger in 1934

The story the body lives in is crazy.
It begins and ends and there is
no end to it but change.

Who was the president in 1934?
Who ran the fastest, held the title?
Who ate radish pudding and green, tinned beef? Who drank
the strong brown god of many beers
behind the canning factory
when their shift was pronounced
dead and dead and over?

Who circled the world in an airplane but lost
his baby to a ladder at the window?

And the rungs of the ladder
that reached so high—you have to believe every one of them
shone with promise and default
like America herself
in 1934. America the beautiful.

I tell you, I have a temper.

It does not mean I have the right to understand it
calmly, or contractually,
as a real estate agent bringing off a deal
for a fixer-upper on a corner lot
with terminal termites—okay—
but what a view!

My father tells a story of 1934.
It is the one I'll tell my shrink
some afternoon when the sun has gone stately
behind the vertical blinds,
and the darkness which ensues is a solid
through a solid,
around a lone *Ficus benjamina*,

and I believe the good doctor has grown fidgety, myself
having bored her to tears . . .

and it goes like this.
Lumped yellow on a bull's eye plate,
it was the squash he wouldn't eat, no thank you. Or the radio
dial

left glowing all night,
until the voice in that disobedient
half-moon named Emerson—how it corresponded
to my father's merciful and true reasons for living

in 1934, with cowboys and pop flies,
the hard out
and Ty Cobb, Ty Cobb,
the long way home though tall grass whistling
Minnie the moocher, she was a lowdown
hootchie-coother.

Either way
he would not apologize.
And my grandmother, a thickset Sicilian woman more frightened
of her anger than angry, or perverse,
would not take no for an answer.

It isn't loss I'm writing about for a change.
It isn't charity begins at home.
Just that when a woman takes her oldest son
to the gates of the local orphanage, hefts him up
(he was light as a feather,
a dog's tear),
to carry him the last
gravel-sounding steps toward county doors
(we do not waste in this house!)

and the boy kicking and convulsing out his terror
with no mama, no, no,
it is one of those moments that bestow upon us
something like hindsight:
acid insight.
Then the knowledge of who and what we are

might last generations,
like the contrail of a great ghost fighter plane,
though we do effectively
nothing ever about it.

Don't get me wrong.
History isn't tyranny.
But the bloodline that begins in said parking lot and ends
in Akron, Ohio,
under the winged boot of Goodyear, the Pope,
and the Soap Box Derby,
what can I say about a family like that?
My father twirling Chianti in Depression glass

has a way of telling stories, I tell you,
it would break your heart.
And my sister catches me
across the mouth again
with the back of her hand—shut up, shut up
and listen.
My brother, Tim,
breaks my brother Patrick's collarbone
inadvertently. And Chuck, grown now,
cannot understand why his wife's son loves him.
Not really, he says, *but the thought*
haunts me sometimes. What keeps us
from hurting something small?

History *isn't* tyranny.
In good arms my grandmother lifted my father up,
arms we recognize immediately
from the memory of people punching bread dough down
as though it were their lives.
But that's another story.

In the one I'm telling today, without benefit of shrink,
a boy is twisting, hiccupping,
pleading, as a feather
bluer than midnight
shimmies on the sensible, raging woman's hat:

No mama, *please.*

What then of the progeny in the wings?
The undetonated cherubs, grandchildren and children
waiting to be born
of the blood of the crying boy himself.
What do they have to say
about all this racket?

I'll give you a clue.
Someone count to ten slowly.
Someone twist in the world like an angel/rat
tensing, stomach to the blow.

❖

Somedays, I see my brothers and sister and I
for what we've always aspired to be.
Ordinary wrecked people.
Not pilots lost fifty-odd years over the Atlantic Ocean
only to be found by some fluke of fate
or clearing weather
and deposited
on a runway in real time,

blinking, disavowed,
still wearing our outdated flak jackets
and our enormous, misguided passions.

Never mind.
The sound of an engine turning over
always rescues the hero in America.
Horselaugh, sputter and catch,
the roar that drowns out
all reasonable doubt:

"Hush, I'd never leave you.
Dio mio, hush; you'll wake the dead."

As if that weren't the point.
Then my father is carried exhausted, faint, compliant, sobbing

—barely able to sob—
back to the waiting Nash
to feel the full weight of good in the world,
of which he now is certain.
Unforsakenness!
It is 1934, you see,
the war has not yet begun.
And we are inside the story
this story lives in, waiting to take our lonely turn.

Hush, I'll never leave you.
Hush, a boy is being gently laid
across the backseat's deep green sea of tufted leather.

Joseph Bathanti

DOMENICO GIUSSEPPE

Singled from the queue filing
through airport security,
my 90 year old father is fully cooperative,
even amiable; not even surprised, it seems,

that fate has tapped him on the shoulder
to answer for something he is innocent of.
Two uniformed buxom matrons,
coiled hair and black patent leather

Sam Browns, heart-shaped
silver badges, ask him
if he's accepted anything from strangers
since he's entered the terminal.

He assures them he never accepts things from strangers.
They study him as if his affability
is part of the ploy, a filament
wired to the bomb he'll trigger.

They prod over him an electric wand,
slip him out of his overcoat, shake his cane.
He smiles and calls them *young lady.*
He's ordered to remove his shoes,

a pair of white Addidas,
not a scuff upon them; and his hat,
an old brown fedora they flip over
and over and empty of its nothingness,

before patting him down like a convict,
armpits and crotch, sliding
their hands up and down his arms and legs,
each skeletal ridge and knob

as if by magic he might divide
and reveal the vault of Armageddon.
Suddenly my father is terrible as Isaiah.
Yet he remains smiling, even as they strip him,

tottering naked on bare yellow feet,
white hair smoking off his chest,
millwright's legs tungsten blue,
from him emanating an audible tick.

Then they peel him out of his skin,
jackknife him open:
sprung, mis-spliced wires,
capped sockets, taped frays –

the mysterious circuitry of detonation.
Still they don't find what they're searching for,
and he can't remember
where he's hidden it.

James Bertolino

DISTRACTED

Today something fell
inside me, I heard it crash.

For a moment I'd been distracted
by the intimacy between

autumn and sunset,
and let go. I don't know

now what I'll do, because
there's a kind of ambush happening

and I've got to save what I can
of who I am.

Raymond L. Bianchi

from AMERICAN MASTER

A delicatessen is a place to buy Jewish cold cuts and pickles
An Italian provision store is a place to buy pork products cured and unavailable to Jews.

Hispanic Groceries have great fruit sections and gross meat sections.

Dim Sum is very expensive …a real rip off.

Chicago has many Polish clubs and there are many Polish intellectuals.

Brazil is hot and humid and everyone wears scanty clothes.

Poets are dishonest about their intentions they only want to meet women.

Bankrolled I put the Roll mop in my mouth and squeeze out its fishy juice.

The best part of Chicago is the poetry reading scene, unless someone from New York is there if that is the case then all the Chicago poets of note will buzz around the NYC poet hoping for favors.

The inquisition was founded to defeat the Catharii in southern
France they were the *perfecti* and believed in purity like the Catholics
—but not the same purity so they were burned alive and purified.

John Brandi

Hymn for a Night Feast

Take the war from me.
Take the penumbra for a crossroad.
Make a parachute from our bedsheets.
Run your hand across the circuit of air
stirred by our bodies.

Take the right and wrong from me.
Take the gleam in the lamb's eye
and wear it as a gown.
Our flesh is counterfeit, fire douses water,
flame spreads the wind.

Take the smoke from my garden.
Take the river as extreme unction.
This room is moist with praise.
A crane lifts its wings
under a canopy of filtered light.

Take what is left and rock the sea.
Take the firefly, the hour hand, the iris.
Make me glorious to the world again.
Give me courage to ask
your name.

Stephen Campiglio

Cause and Effect

Camped outside the door,
the persistent stray that insists on a home
charges the opening.

Although I stop the cat with both hands,
it keeps coming and gets through my legs.

The commotion doesn't seem to bother my father.
He's in the kitchen, his respite from the dead.
He looks younger since he died

and doesn't say a word,
wiping the counter top dry.

Then a car pulls into the driveway
and the tires crackle on the gravel.
I scamper outside, but there's only

the cat triumphant in the window,
my father neatly squaring the kitchen rag.

Kara Candito

POSTCARD: I'VE BEEN MEANING TO WRITE—

because it's August in an ancient city and I want to
tell you about this heat that hangs like the mind

of a landscape in which everything is still and irritable
as the stray cats that nap on the ruins of Pompey's theatre.

Because the man who served my espresso this morning
looked like you. In a certain light, I peered through

the bronze keyhole and saw the Basilica framed by fire.
Because I miss you even as I try to efface you,

like the lunatic who smashed David's genitals with a hammer.
Beauty is an anesthesia here. It dulls the brain. I write;

it's called memory, then story. It never resembles the real
things I want to say when the wind is still and fountains

rush around the night. My apartment is dark and laundry
hangs in sad heaps on the balcony. There are chicken bones

in the sink. Below, in the Piazza, a *gelateria.* At night,
families arrive—men holding their sons high, like props;

women blowing smoke in imperfect circles and whispering
behind manicured hands about their husbands' affairs.

So many minor betrayals (the urge to sleep through church bells).
The Triumph of Galatea, on the reverse, is short and coarse.

Recall that it ends in bloodshed. I think Raphael understood
that no one wants to be Polyphemus, the one who sees

her eyes as little spurs in his sides and suffers and hides.
We all want to be Galatea, laughing sidelong, smirking

over her shoulder at a suitor's clumsy song. Such a small
offense. And doesn't it make her beautiful? So, grief becomes

the punishment for ridicule and justice is its own rapture—
a boulder hurled, a river pounding a hollow cave in the head.

I can't forget your studio, the one on the side street,
with sealed windows. Everything inside cheap and new

or abandoned and broken. On the wall, a still life of overripe
fruit in a wooden frame. How you envied the voluptuous grapes,

the way they burst over the rim of the bowl—

David Cappella

The Clothespin

La vita è triste ed io son solo.
—Dino Campana

The clothespin hangs on the gray line
Halfway between the stolid oak and the house.

I see an orange angel, perched like a bird,
Solitary, still, as snow falls straight down.

Its presence sags slightly in my mind,
Suspended, as though caught away from heaven,

It has decided to endure winter's mortal grip.
An angel? I ask myself gazing out at it

From the kitchen window. Why an angel?
Angels do not visit a man alone at home,

One relaxed in the fears of his life.
I have noticed the pin since early fall: in slippers,

Naked after a shower, opening a bottle of wine.
But I have never noticed an angel in the backyard.

The house is empty. I think that I am terrified.
The wind is on the rise. I hear its deep yearning.

There is nowhere to hide in this world, except the self.
And the strains of love are nowhere to be found.

In winter, there is nothing left,
Except icy stars staring down, tense,

Waiting for me to stare up at them,
To grasp my longing, to endure this vision

Of beauty that provokes distracted eyes.
It is dusk. I lean over the kitchen sink,

Strain to eye the clothespin, indifferent
To the snow, my gaze, and all suffering.

So, I turn away and leave the clothespin on the line.

Emanuel Carnevali

ITALIAN FARMER

Years of bending to his spade
have cast a weight upon him, so that he is
hunchback.
The patches of his pants (for hardly ever does he wear a jacket)
form the most ridiculous and yet the most tragic
flag. His shirt
is unspeakably dirty.

The earth, that damn stepmother,
has sucked his flesh
so that he is a mass of contracted muscles.
His gnarled face, where no human feelings can be discerned,
is a mask of many sorrows, much pain and no vanity at all.
The sun and the moon he never knew or saw
for he never lifted his face to the sky.
Sky is merely the recipient of rain for him,
sky is the place where an improbable God sits doing nothing;
stars are things that make little light;
the sun is what scorches him in the summer and what makes
little heat in the winter.
He bends down to the earth and asks for nothing:
knowing too well the earth is a traitor which gives and does not
give. His songs are unbeautiful, for songs mean laziness
and this farmer would die if he didn't work.

Wine cannot kill him or give him peace.
His drunkenness is as black as his soberness.
Drunkenness of no laughter, dark, drunkenness of damnation.
Drunkenness that is near to death.
Silent he is but no sphinx,
his sorrow is plain enough; in fact
it is often paltry too.
When he is drunk he sings songs that have
the sadness of an ass braying.
He has no great sorrow because his soul is small,
but he resents the darkness of his soul, for that
eats at his heart like the philoxera that eats
the roots of the grape trees.
What if his fields are beautiful in the sun,
what if his grapes weigh sometimes five kilo to a bunch,
he thinks only what he has to gain by all of them,
and a veil of ugliness descends at once over them all for his eyes to see.
He knows the rage of seeing that the earth does not respond to his care.
He knows the despair after a thunderstorm that brings with it
the terrible all-destroying hail.

Hardly ever is he religious,
considering, not wrongly I think, that religion
is a thing for women and children.
Love is too delicate an affair for him,
and women are damnable and useless.

Christine Casson

GRACE

Gnats swarm in the red shaft of lowering
sun, a chaos of dives, swirls towering
as we circumvent the frenzied cloud
to the patio, settle in a garden chair
just out of their way, wrought-iron flowers
at our backs. This dance of confusion
could have sprung from the fuss of a human day,
the endless ring of cell phones, car alarms,
avalanche of emails with *something* to say,
a gaggle of information from circling
memos, voicemail, the TV's non-stop prattle.

Our bergamot launches high and purple
in deepening air, its rich stain refashioned
in shadows that pool the cooling ground,
and one last bee hums hungrily around petals
spiked wide by steady heat, an alluring runway
to the pollinated core, sticky sweet,
drenched in secret scent. The seduction
is hesitant at first, a taste, another sip,
a meditative hovering, and then the diving in.
The flower's head bows ever so slightly,
a tremor runs the length of its stiff stem.

On the patio we sit and talk (the day
still well-lit near its end) of daily things: work, home,
my mother growing old—where will she live?—
the meal we'll prepare together. We savor
our wine to the gnats' buzz, the quieting street,
the turning in, rise and fall of our murmured speech
like those million small black flecks lifting—a sail
lightly stirred by air. We hadn't seen before
how they shift, spin awry, away, and then reverse,
a fluid thrumming cell drawn back to the pattern
of a beat that sways and sings beyond our measure.

Grace Cavalieri

Father

When I see the 1900's walk by
        in early frock coat from a former time
I see you in grey and brown like
        New York, its cold cement,
Small canisters of milk carried
        downstairs by children
Who could not speak the language;
        I hear the chicken freezing
In your yard, let loose so
        you could eat that night.
And of the pack of you,
        squabbling and squawking in the corner
No regard is given by your
        Queen Mother sitting in the
Chair, embroidering her dream of
        Florence where there were
Stables, the town apartment
        in Venice, the fields to the
North around Pisa, sewing the colors she knew
        on fine silk.

When I think of your father, the professor
        coming home, without money, paid once more
In love and adulation by the crowds,
        in their dialect
And how he died with pennies on his eyelids,
        the secret note speaking
Of his failures to you, my father, the eldest,
        did you know
Where to go with that pain? How ashamed
        you must be of us;
Your brother's sons are physicians, physicists
        researching the stars
And he, eighteen months younger than you,
        spared again.

Joseph Ceravolo

The Green Lake Is Awake

Part I

The womb can
remind you of mosquitoes
if you imagine you are
in a carriage with a net
over it

A negro is shining the
top of a used car. The pennant
is above him.

Where are you? Here I am
crossing the street. This is
my mommy. O sun!

A dog walks over to the
little boy. He walks over
sideways and bashful.
The boy throws a rock to him

The shell goes around and the
car turns over. The sunlight
is as clear as a
green bottle.

Man walking with his
shoulders haunched and tufts
of white duck hair in the back
of the head! where were you born

The day is like splattered glass
The girls are wearing
bright sweaters and blouses.
They stop to let the cars pass

Life is green. Love is gray.
Purple are girls going to
school in wine jackets.

You stand at the corner of two
walls. Like handball
courts and a big bee
flies around you

There are many trees around
here. A bird flies crazily
to one.
Will he
go in or not?

A group of boys are waiting
to go in a yellow bus. A bird
down below flies over the
wall past me. Its front is blazing.

        I am walking slowly. My feet
won't move. A Rheingold truck
drives past me.

        Rosemary is drinking
tea. Paul is running in his
sunsuit. The phone separates
        us. They are eternal.
                        The phone is hot.

If you can imagine
a park, then you can
        see this crushed lollipop.

Part 2

I feel the cold peach
in my pocket. I am not
wearing a sweater.

        Advance as I come to
you!   Alcohol comes to us.

Open your hand; the
fly springs away. The
air is cool on this spring-
board. The water must be cool.

Paul is watching me. His
eyes get sleepy with intensity.
He looks like he's
going to sneeze.

A whale was swimming near the coast last night.
The cement truck turns and I
realize how totally abandoned
all these workers are in their
easy happiness. But are they in
a combination of the wind?
I was looking all over for
                    you.

Summer Dragon

A woman is walking. Her dress
is green as the grass and as
surprising. She has a hunched
back and her hair is
        gray like autumn grass
            and she walks
        looking down along the
grass lost and penetrating.
Is autumn

A Song

        Why am I so dumb
now that you're gone;
now that you are gone?

The trucks behind me are
going at blasting power
A man walks toward
        me. The sun is blasting
the green shiny weeds
that are all around
                There is no one on the
                road. The road curves.
                I can't see where it goes
                    The bushes move but
                    the telephone pole doesn't

The roller goes over the
asphalt. The song "Love where
are you now, now that I need
you so" comes to me.
The roller goes over.
        But the rain falls down
and tatters away
my balls.

The whistle blows.
        Where are you now?
People cross the street
They are all carrying something.

        What is this half feeding?
This half happiness
that hops at me

last night?
We picked you up last night
and you were beautiful,
the internal sunset
after the darkness
has stopped moving.
The plant that emits
a fragrance with all mothers.

In you, I feel
the new kite.
What are your feelings
like?

O chemical and possible
flash, The song goes
on and on; the song.

Part 3

No mine is like
the presents I want
to give you:
wet lips, solar aches,
roadway dust, and
the rays of the moon
at the spots where they start.
I was born

before both of you
but like a man
I'm being withered
by you both
                    into the dust
          of the moon
that you have brought
          back on your feet.
I see you both
and I am dispersed
like clouds mixing
like children skating.

Working writing and
decorating this star bright
misery.   This pure
and lovely porto rican
waist.   Where do
they work?

          The little boys are fishing.
Just concentrating on hearing.
A sound of wheels squeaking
is in the trees.
Forever the sound goes on
like crickets, like night or
birds that call along
the highway and are barely
seen.

How long can I sit here?
Rest! The night is
being held by
light droplets

Ride your bicycle, my negro
green as the lake and
black as the trunks of trees.

I hear the train. I am
calling to the lake. "Goodbye."
I turned my head fast.
I thought it was you at
a glance.
But it was a lady
carrying a fishing net.
She's younger than I thought.

A group of people touch
me. What a life!
What a saw!
Charge me! oh silent
zoo-bird.

I walk around this
leaf falling park
Will I meet
someone I know, so far away?

Am I a Part of this
wheel of matter? just
because I am made of matter?
            I too disappear like solids;
. . . . .tomorrow night.
                The green lake is awake

        There are brown leaves
on the ground
        but I don't see even one
        in the full trees.

I was born a fluid.
The sun is shining on
half of the sign "Steel Pier."
        Magnifying.

        The white duck is
blue along the water.
It skates slowly
        back and forth far
from me.
                My head will be warm
            because the air is warmer
            than the water.

I will see the duck like a baby
                coming towards me.

Part 4

It is time to go
        Love me! even when I falter.
The autumn leaves are
now beginning to start
falling.

I am awake: like
a colloid
just discovered in
            a breeze.

The truck woke me up.
            Assembling outside.
Two birds fly
over the street. They are on their way to some
        food. People are
continuing into their
building, to work.
        How friendly are
        those birds to
        each other?

The bee is coming closer to me.
It is like a flying object.

The duck is bobbing up and down.
It stays almost

in the same spot
as the water under it
moves away like a river.

The leaves are falling only when the wind blows.
I have five minutes.

How I would like to just fall
asleep. . . . . . . .in the
movement . . . . .of all this
. . . . . . with you
near by me as I stretch
out my arm . . . . . .
          with all these leaves
rolling across
                    each other
Ditto, what suffering.
Accumulation.
Love,
degeneration, . . .
and regenerated dives

Every man or woman has
his own generator of love.

                              This autumn,
                              this autumn.
                                 beard,
                              this autumn.

The crack in the wall
goes to the left
then to the right
continues down.
It stares at me.
It stares at us.
Paul is with us, you
are with us.
The stars are uncontrollable.

A woman is walking. The
muscles in her legs are
moving in slow gulps.
The gym comes
to my mind and the
smell at the beginning.
It's
so
early.

Part 5

There's a match on
the floor; O bathroom of
stages! The sun burns through
the glass. It fortifies
the density of the leaves
and of your crying
last night.

I saw three girls
passing, going to work,
yet the whole street is
moving away.
The acorns are dry
The acorns are green
on the inside. . . .
resonant as
a testicle.

Oh cars, south breeze, two
people standing facing, truck,
baseball bat, swing, lint
flying around,
go! on on on

Evening,
I am holding the
ball, evening.

There is a new kite.
It is a bird kite.
It looks like a
bird.
It is made of stretched plastic.
No bird can
fly forever without
moving its wings.
The kite does not move
its wings.
But there is a noise coming from it

The electric motor new and
used is not like our brain
here in the darkness,
here in the morning black.
Take-ah, take-ah, tant, tant
          do-ah, do-ah
The bird goes in a tree.
        Bird goes
The bird goes
The pointed wings of
the seagulls
        practice on
pumping the skies.

                Orange soda.
                Distant voices.

        How different each acorn
        is here in his hand
        here in the light, here in the
park   here in the light;
how different each
crumb is here in
          its beak

John Ciardi

Back

On the mountain after Vesuvius
in what I have left
of the dialect I started from,
I sit with unknown cousins.

Except for the Alfa Romeo
nosing the mayor's house,
a fluorescence of TV reflected
in the glass of an open door,
and the monument to the war dead,
we could choose at a whim
what century we sit to.

We have red wine, bread, *pecorino,*
fave, and garlicky olives before us.
A table set in Pompeii.

Below, at the cliff of San Barbato,
the bearded saint, is the stump
of the Lombard tower my name
came here to in the tenth century,
having crossed the Alps with Alboin
four hundred years earlier
as Gerhardt.

I explain
what I have read. They nod respect
that I have read a book.

How he came clanging in 568
allied with Saxons, the conquered
Gedidae sworn to him. Rosamund,
daughter of their murdered king,
his slave queen till 572, when—
all of high Italy under his axe—
she cut his throat to vengeance
for having had a wine bowl
made from her father's skull
and forcing her to drink.

. . .They know the blood of history.
They drink it to fable
and fill the glass again.

A cousin asks, "Was there
a son of that marriage
and was he king after?"

"No. Cleph succeeded.
A chief of another line."
He sips. "It is better so.
But who was Gerhardt?"

...An unknown axe-clanger,

the name changed to Gherardi
on his sons' new tongue,
and that to Cerardi
by the time it reached here
some Lombard lordling later,
and again to Ciardi
as, round the mountain
at San Potito Ultra, my fathers
spoke it eight hundred years
till its last sound there
moved to Dover, New Jersey.

They nod. They, too, have names
from these same marches.
Though not my mother—none
she could follow. De Benedictis—
"Of the Blessed"—a church gift
to a foundling at old doors,
its shadow mother
gone to forgotten sorrows, the name
already a thousand year line
in the one furrow it lived from.

On father stones we sit drinking.
The men have bad teeth and loud voices.
Their hands are knobbed
as if by broken knuckles. Haft hands
axed from harder wood than grows here.
The women stand behind us

where the Greeks left them.
When the bottle is empty
they bring another.
                                        We talk.
Enough of history. It has been said.
We say nothing. Nothing is necessary.
The wine, the food, the sitting to it
is what there is to say. We say
the wine is good. The *pecorino*
is good. And what olives! Here,
taste this spumanti that I made
myself. Could you buy
a wine like that? Could you?

I am fat, soft-handed,
and have tickets in my pocket—
a choice of oceans.
I am from the miracle
great-uncles left for a century back
leaving them what land there was
to break the knobs of their hands on.

I am of my wristwatch
as they are of sun-up.
                                        We talk.
The women the Greeks left
bring us wine and twilight.
Indoors the children watch TV
and the image shimmers

on the glass of an open door.
The mayor's son waves and goes by.
It grows dark.
We sit in whatever century we are left in.
The wine is good. The *pecorino*
is good. The *fave* and the olives
are good.

David Citino

VOLARE

Just as lights inside our living room
and steam from water boiling on the stove
erase Cleveland from the picture window,
father comes in,
stands in the kitchen, one shoulder thrust forward,
feet apart the way he's seen Lanza stand,
eyelids drooping like Dean Martin's or Como's,
Lucky Strike stuck to lower lip.
We can leave the confusion
and all disillusion behind.
And we know he got the raise,
his laborer's share of chemical company profits
from the Manhattan Project
and the revolution in plastics.
Four hundred a year. And that's not hay.
He grabs my mother
and spins with her before the stove,
wooden spoon brandished like the fine lady's fan
she saw that day in pages of *Life.*
Just like birds of a feather
a rainbow together we'll find.
Then he comes for me,
and I'm soaring above cauldrons
of rigatoni and sauce bubbling bright

as the scarlet cassocks altar boys wear
at Christmas and Easter.
He brings me back to earth
and twirls away to phone his mother.
That night when he comes home from moonlighting
in the credit department at Sears,
feet heavy as bricks,
he'll come to my bedroom and tell me again
how there'll be no promotion for him
because he couldn't go to college
but still he's risen higher than his father
who put in fifty years with the B & O.
He'll step out the door
and for a moment his head will be caught in light
like some raptured hoary saint drunk on love
in the window of Ascension of Our Lord
and the last thing I'll hear
will be his lovely forlorn baritone
fading, falling into stillness.
Volare. Wo-wo. Cantare. Wo-o-o-o.

Ned Condini

Saint Vincent Ferrer, New York

They overtake me, cursing through their spit
taxicabs' din in the skyscrapers' canyons —
the most deafening city in the world.
'Twas there I saw, on Seventy-First Street
and Madison, a slim Madonna, a girl
dressed in crimson and white open the portals
to a brown, imposing church. I followed her,
Petrarch enchanted by Madonna Laura.
The young girl held the door ajar for me.
I tiptoed in, slowly opening my eyes
to aisles and naves and frescoes on the walls,
a vaulted dome, a miracle of huge
blue stained-glass windows that suddenly made me
enthusiastic to ascend to heaven
with Laura at my side. But she had gone
to Our Lady's chapel to kneel down and pray.

The windows flared with mauves, violets, purples,
and their dark beauty blinded me for moments.
When I regained my sight, I contemplated
the awesome blue in veneration, gliding
down from the vault to massive pillars, walls
adorned with paintings showing the Via Crucis
in its dolorous steps which I retraced

until my eyes met with a golden radiance
that struck me like a child's storybook: Christ's
first fall under the burden of the cross.
A desolating scene but, to my wonder,
the face seemed to be smiling in its fall.
Pick up your cross — the smile invited me.

At that instant, a monk I couldn't see
started to play the organ — chords from Bach.
Like an adoring Wise Man I continued
my pilgrimage along the cross's path
looking this time for the Madonna I had
glimpsed in the chapel just as she was lighting
a votive candle, pointing out the way
from foolish pride to Mary bowed by pain
in front of the mauled body of her son —
she was not there. The music from the organ
reached a crescendo, the cross above the altar
through Jesus' twisted shape reiterated
pick up your cross, be unperturbed in trouble.

Reluctantly I stepped out of the church,
Vincent Ferrer casting glee on *my* face,
into a bracing wind. The sky was blue,
a stained-glass window mirroring the earth,
and, below, people walking in its glow.
The day bloomed back, redeemed, with me in love
again with bustling streets, with men and women
stumbling along, doggedly looking for

innocence, expiation and renewal:
blue sky, purity of white, gold of the cross.
Back to the sanctity of my room, I, Petrarch,
gathered the pieces of my broken soul
restored to unity by Vincent and
with Laura in mind and heart sat down and wrote.

Gregory Corso

Italian Extravaganza

Mrs. Lombardi's month-old son is dead.
I saw it in Rizzo's funeral parlor.
A small purplish wrinkled head.

They've just finished having high mass for it;
They're coming out now
. . . wow, such a small coffin!
And ten black cadillacs to haul it in.

Paolo Corso

The Doctor Makes His Diagnosis

I have two cities but only one home

that is my mother's womb
with one long umbilical cord
that reaches across thousands
of frequent flyer miles.

I have two apartments and one window

filled with pleats of light
and a sooty curtain
that no matter the color
is a checkered gray.

I have "an abiding devotion" to my birthplace,

so when I go back to Pittsburgh,
I'm *stupida* for living in Brooklyn
and when I'm living in Brooklyn,
I'm mad with longing.

I have an "afflicted imagination"

that incapacitates my body, causing
nausea, loss of appetite, high fever,
pathological changes in the lungs,
brain inflammation and cardiac arrest.

I have a "lifeless and haggard countenance,"

an "idleness conducive to daydreaming"
about thick village milk and Iron City beer,
about the sounds of bagpipes and Terrible Towels
whipping in stadium winds.

I have three college degrees and seven bookcases

but rely solely on "associationist magic."
When I climb the stairs to the torch
of the Statue of Liberty, I imagine being
at the top of an idle factory smokestack.

I have a "highly contagious disease" but curable

if you purge my stomach, induce torture and pain.
I can be ridiculed, laughed out of my homesickness
unless you see me as a working-class woman
who does a white-collar job with blue-collar hands.

Gerald Costanzo

The White Experience in America

From the beginning
we were reared on the power
of illusion: Freedom:
Justice: Mannikins dressed
to resemble Hayley Mills

and Dean Jones
wrested from the fiery
train wrecks of the cinema.
Give us the Roseland Roller
Rink, the Tivoli, and Acme

Arcade. The Brothers at Glastonbury
Abbey on any October morning
rising to pray. Drunks at the curb
in front of the bank on Vine
Street, where the men

with jackhammers are taking
a break. The diesel will save us.
The all-nite diner. Tell us
the truth about Jersey City
or Woonsocket and we will rage

in letters to the editor.

Remind us of witch hunts
and we will claim no credit
for the past, then admit
we have always been prepared

to give violence its chance.
Listen, what we've believed
is solid and manageable
like a thumbprint
or the College of Hard Knocks.

Peter Covino

WELLINGTON DINER INFIDEL

Easter morning, sitting in a beige vinyl seat.
I had just outed myself, distanced
Myself from so many things I wanted.

Cast away from the comforts of lamb shank
And relatives, my parents whispering
With the shame of me. Holy Week, and no one

To call family, not unholy, but reluctant,
Woozy as a newborn giraffe, crouched there
Beneath the knobby knees of its mother

Who's just delivered, from six feet above.
And each step, because in this life I'm born
Again, feels like a conversation in

A mysterious language. This new, stuttered
Existence, so far from the *Kyries*
And the thirteenth station in the church

Of my youth, named after St. Roch, healer,
Patron saint of the sick, especially
Revered in this Italian neighborhood

(Rocco, a name common as John.) It was
There that words first saved me, prayers to some
Sanctimonious muse. A surrogate

God-mother I spoke to again earlier
Today, when that familiar void overwhelmed me—
As it did that night on the edge of twenty

And suicide, when the parish priest,
Father Della Rosa, came to the house
And commanded in barely passable

English: "No matter what, God loves you."
Right about now in Rome, in the square
Of the saint I'm named after, namesake also

Of my grandfather, pilgrims begin to
Shuffle in—I can almost touch them through
The diner window—busloads full, from

Uganda, Brazil, Papua New Guinea.
Placards and whistles of tour guides excite
The air. Men, children, and mostly women

Crossing the threshold of the basilica,
The journey of a lifetime culminating
In this one rapturous moment. Some burst

Into tears, saving waters rushing over;
Others swoon, needing to be revived,
Slapped back—into this merciful life.

Pellegrino D'Acierno

Warning

I feel that life's perpetual fight goes on,
Treacherous, cruel, foolish, merciless,
For I see that the weak is ever won
By the mighty one, and thus made helpless.

Of an infinite throng I hear the moan,
Silent moan, which no word can yet explain,
Though it swells in the soul, till bursts alone,
Like anger kindled by a racking pain.

. . . Some day I shall hear no more that lament
Which now, O potent, carries utter joys
To your soul coward, mean and insolent:

But the plebs, blind no more to your outrage,
Shall arise and with its virile, roaring voice
Shall crush at once your sinister image.

Pascal D'Angelo

THE TOILERS

Brown faces of immature senility
Twisted into an ecstasy of unshaped satiation.
Eyes that are huge, tumultuous flares of light
Peering athwart the forced austerity of tiredness.
Your hugely-muscled, stalwart arms
That lift the mammoth weight of majestic industry,
Branch up from your broad Herculean shoulders
In a magnificence of thronged power.
Reeling on the verge of eagerness
You shift about—
Throughout the night you are hurled
In a confused heave of struggling illusions,
Under the machinal flights of those moistened
        walls,
Under those black, moistened walls of disregarded
        futility.
Facing this Giant monument of bitterness —
Your thoughts!
Amid the incessant whirrs of the maniac motors,
Are smashed into fragments of an irresolved
        dream,
And you are swept on! On!
By the involuntary rapids of meniality
In frenzied whirls of humiliation!
On! On!

Rachel Guido deVries

Italian Grocer

After he was produce manage for the A & P,
Pop opened his own store. He polished apples
to lay alongside sweet Jersey peaches all
fuzzy and gold, and sometimes got figs which he
held up like gems. Bread and baccala, olives
in a big brown barrel. Provolone, locatelli,
Genoa salami, prosciutto behind a gleaming
case. Each morning he donned a white coat
like a doctor, marched the aisles, and watched.

He hired Angie the dyke to keep things neat.
She fed me cherries when I was three. Mamma
worried I'd choke. Pop and Angie laughed
and Angie said I'd learn what to do
with those pits.

When the store burned, Pop went mad and wept
all over the street. Angie vanished from me, and
the queer man upstairs lost all of his drag. White
people in the neighborhood said Pop the Wop
torched his own store for insurance. He had none.
His white coat, smelling of cheese and fish,
was gone.

Ray DiPalma

from Provocations

Then the language doesn't get used up

A bent crowd

Inside language

Nor is it bluer or hybrid

Wrapped in time-honored bars of light

The work of a mason and a nomad

THE ONUS IN NOUNS

What happens within the progress of thought when words
Are applied
What happens against the progress of thought when words
Are applied

Tilth thorn and thistle
The sky in the pond

Curious expression: dead for a while
Which way does it face
What does it *expect*

Hearing what was said in the moment of memory
What was said did not originate with the sayer
Made the memory made out of words

Hearing what the memory made
Saying what the hearing that the memory made

The sky is never invisible whatever is held or planned against it. With contact the sky is always a place to start. While waiting and so acknowledge waiting ideas eventually come, almost erasing the flawed initiative of the past and deepening the crease between the eyes and just above the bridge of the nose.

Ja, Qui Da, Yes, Si . . . the soil is pause from place to soil: *to place from place* and *place to place.* Flat stones at the entrance of the tunnel. Separation in the ink.

Diane di Prima

Backyard

where angels turned into honeysuckle & poured nectar into my mouth
where I French-kissed the roses in the rain
where demons tossed me a knife to kill my father in the stark
    simplicity of the sky
where I never cried
where all the roofs were black
where no one opened the venetian blinds
O Brooklyn! Brooklyn!
where fences crumbled under the weight of rambling roses
and naked plaster women bent eternally white over birdbaths
the icicles on the chains of the swings tore my fingers
& the creaking tomato plants tore my heart as they wrapped their
    roots around fish heads rotting beneath them
& the phonograph too creaked Caruso come down from the skies;
    Tito Gobbi in gondola; Gigli ridiculous in soldier uniform;
    Lanza frenetic
& the needle tore at the records & my fingers
tore poems into little pieces & watched the sky
where clouds torn into pieces & livid w/neon or rain
scudded away from Red Hook, away from Gowanus Canal, away
from Brooklyn Navy Yard where everybody worked, to fall to pieces
    over Clinton Street
and the plaster saints in the yard never looked at the naked women
    in the birdbaths

and the folks coming home from work in pizza parlor or furniture
    store, slamming wrought iron gates to come
    upon brownstone houses,
never looked at either: they saw that the lawns were dry
were eternally parched beneath red gloomy sunsets we viewed from
a thousand brownstone stoops
leaning together by thousands on the same
wrought-iron banister, watching the sun impaled
on black St. Stephen's steeple

John Domini

LAKESHORE, L.A., LONG ISLAND, EX-O-SKEL.

Always this beach thing. When, I mean,
it's serious, whatever brought me there.
Chicago, interviewing (hey, at least
the snowstorm meant those bastards had to put
me up an extra night)…still I crabbed
across Lakeshore, as if I needed this,
my face shellacked, my legs humiliated.
As if I needed this, graffiti sky,
the crust off bitter Michigan.

Or better weather, City of the Angels.
I drove the length of Santa Monica,
the stoplights off their moorings in the sun.
In Beverly Hills we'd made a handshake deal
that left infection crawling up my arm,
I maxxed the Visa, missed the rental-Benz
return, and all I had to go on was
the name: a Boulevard that ended at
a Pier. Sand itself seemed disinfectant,
abrasive, cleansing, flecked. I wished I was
pure *Angeleno,* baptized, sweet-tongued, sure
of the proverb: *El mar cura todos.*

Connecticut seems stranger yet. The shore
sink-porcelain, smeared with shavings, off beyond

the glass. There'd been nothing doing at
the conference in the city, nothing, yet
its final night — lucky me, and where
I'd least expected luck. A woman who
I'd always wanted. Her tiara shed
its glitter on the windows of the train,
the New Year's speckle winking in the smear
of coast. In our reflected eager smut.

Colonial w/ vu of Sound, her score,
house-sitting till the bubble bulged again.
Pretending we were rich, pretending we
had promise, we undid each other, there
before the windows. Different windows, these,
antiques, hand-blown, the whorls a blessing, really —
encrypting our sags and wrinkles. Outside,
the sand and weed-scrap blurred the hummocks, keening.
A couple days of that, and then I'm on
the bus, I'm heading for La Guardia.
Whatever bridge we took, to me it seemed
the same: illegible. The diesel grime,
the tinted plexiglass: plain murk, that's all,
my weekend luck, my kingdom by the sea.

I wondered how it looked from her end, if
it read more prettily. Jonah might be nice,
delivered from Leviathan. But all
my seaside fables come in code, shell games
abandoned when the kids are rounded up.
An exoskelo-echo, snatch of bugle.

Elaine Equi

MULBERRY STREET

It's the kind of street
that would be behind
one of those crooners
who sang on TV in the 1950s.

A streetlamp, a cemetery
and a big full moon.
What more could a person
want or need?

O to live on nothing
but arugula and espresso,
forever doing penance
in that somber church
across the street.

The one that's surrounded
by a wall that leans on you
as much as you lean on it.

The one full of flickering lights
and statues that talk.
"The dead," they say.
"The dead will outlive us all."

Lawrence Ferlinghetti

Autobiography

I am leading a quiet life
in Mike's Place every day
watching the champs
of the Dante Billiard Parlor
and the French pinball addicts.
I am leading a quiet life
on lower East Broadway.
I am an American.
I was an American boy.
I read the American Boy Magazine
and became a boy scout
in the suburbs.
I thought I was Tom Sawyer
catching crayfish in the Bronx River
and imagining the Mississippi.
I had a baseball mit
and an American Flyer bike.
I delivered the Woman's Home Companion
at five in the afternoon
or the Herald Trib
at five in the morning.
I still can hear the paper thump
on lost porches.
I had an unhappy childhood.
I saw Lindberg land.

I looked homeward
and saw no angel. I got caught stealing pencils
from the Five and Ten Cent Store
the same month I made Eagle Scout.
I chopped trees for the CCC
and sat on them.
I landed in Normandy
in a rowboat that turned over.
I have seen the educated armies
on the beach at Dover.
I have seen Egyptian pilots in purple clouds
shopkeepers rolling up their blinds
at midday
potato salad and dandelions
at anarchist picnics.
I am reading 'Lorna Doone'
and a life of John Most
terror of the industrialist
a bomb on his desk at all times.
I have seen the garbagemen parade
in the Columbus Day Parade
behind the glib
farting trumpeters.
I have not been out to the Cloisters
in a long time
nor to the Tuileries
but I still keep thinking
of going.
I have seen the garbagemen parade
when it was snowing.

I have
eaten hotdogs in ballparks.
I have heard the Gettysburg Address
and the Ginsbeg Address.
I like it here
and I won't go back
where I came from.
I too have ridden boxcars boxcars boxcars.
I have travelled among unknown men.
I have been in Asia
with Noah in the Ark.
I was in India
when Rome was built.
I have been in the Manger
with an Ass.
I have seen the Eternal distributor
from a White Hill
in South San Francisco
and the Laughing Woman at Loona Park
outside the Fun House
in a great rainstorm
still laughing.
I have heard the sound of revelry
by night.
I have wandered lonely
as a crowd.
I am leading a quiet life
outside of Mike's Place every day
watching the world walk by
in its curious shoes.

I once started out
to walk around the world
but ended up in Brooklyn.
That Bridge was too much for me.
I have engaged in silence
exile and cunning.
I flew too near the sun
and my wax wings fell off.
I am looking for my Old Man
whom I never knew.
I am looking for the Lost Leader
with whom I flew.
Young men should be explorers.
Home is where one starts from.
But Mother never told me
there'd be scenes like this.
Womb-weary
I rest
I have travelled.
I have seen goof city.
I have seen the mass mess.
I have heard Kid Ory cry.
I have heard a trombone preach.
I have heard Debussy
strained thru a sheet.
I have slept in a hundred islands
where books were trees.
I have heard the birds
that sound like bells.
I have worn grey flannel trousers

and walked upon the beach of hell.
I have dwelt in a hundred cities
where trees were books.
What subways what taxis what cafes!
What women with blind breasts
limbs lost among skyscrapers!
I have seen the statues of heroes
at carrefours.
Danton weeping at a metro entrance
Columbus in Barcelona
pointing Westward up the Ramblas
toward the American Express
Lincoln in his stony chair
And a great Stone Face
in North Dakota.
I know that Columbus
did not invent America.
I have heard a hundred housebroken Ezra Pounds.
They should all be freed.
It is long since I was a herdsman.
I am leading a quiet life
in Mike's Place every day
reading the Classified columns.
I have read the Reader's Digest
from cover to cover
and noted the close identification
of the United States and Promised Land
where every coin is marked
In God We Trust
but the dollar bills do not have it

being gods unto themselves.
I read the Want Ads daily
looking for a stone a leaf
an unfound door.
I hear America singing
in the Yellow Pages.
One could never tell
the soul has its rages.
I read the papers every day
and hear humanity amiss
in the sad plethora of print.
I see where Walden Pond has been drained
to make an amusement park.
I see they're making Melville
eat his whale.
I see another war is coming
but I won't be there to fight it.
I have read the writing
on the outhouse wall.
I helped Kilroy write it.
I marched up Fifth Avenue
blowing on a bugle in a tight platoon
but hurried back to the Casbah
looking for my dog.
I see a similarity
between dogs and me.
Dogs are the true observers
walking up and down the world
thru the Molloy country.
I have walked down alleys

too narrow for Chryslers.
I have seen a hundred horseless milkwagons
in a vacant lot in Astoria.
Ben Shahn never painted them
but they're there
askew in Astoria.
I have heard the junkman's obbligato.
I have ridden superhighways
and believed the billboard's promises
Crossed the Jersey Flats
and seen the Cities of the Plain
And wallowed in the wilds of Westchester
with its roving bands of natives
in stationwagons.
I have seen them.
I am the man.
I was there.
I suffered
somewhat.
I am an American.
I have a passport.
I did not suffer in public.
And I'm too young to die.
I am a selfmade man.
And I have plans for the future.
I am in line
for a top job.
I may be moving on
to Detroit.
I am only temporarily

a tie salesman.
I am a good Joe.
I am an open book
to my boss.
I am a complete mystery
to my closest friends.
I am leading a quiet life
in Mike's Place every day
contemplating my navel.
I am a part
of the body's long madness.
I have wandered in various nightwoods.
I have leaned in drunken doorways.
I have written wild stories
without punctuation.
I am the man.
I was there.
I suffered
somewhat.
I have sat in an uneasy chair.
I am a tear of the sun.
I am a hill
where poets run.
I invented the alphabet
after watching the flight of cranes
who made letters with their legs.
I am a lake upon a plain.
I am a word
in a tree.
I am a hill of poetry.

I am a raid
on the inarticulate.
I have dreamt
that all my teeth fell out
but my tongue lived
to tell the tale.
For I am a still
of poetry.
I am a bank of song.
I am a playerpiano
in an abandoned casino
on a seaside esplanade
in a dense fog
still playing.
I see a similarity
between the Laughing Woman
and myself.
I have heard the sound of summer
in the rain.
I have seen girls on boardwalks
have complicated sensations.
I understand their hesitations.
I am a gatherer of fruit.
I have seen how kisses
cause euphoria.
I have risked enchantment.
I have seen the Virgin
in an appletree at Chartres
and Saint Joan burn
at the Bella Union.

I have seen giraffes in junglejims
their necks like love
wound around the iron circumstances
of the world.
I have seen the Venus Aphrodite
armless in her drafty corridor.
I have heard a siren sing
at One Fifth Avenue.
I have seen the White Goddess dancing
in the Rue des Beaux Arts
on the Fourteenth of July
and the Beautiful Dame Without Mercy
picking her nose in Chumley's.
She did not speak English.
She had yellow hair
and a hoarse voice
and no bird sang.
I am leading a quiet life
in Mike's Place every day
watching the pocket pool players
making the minestrone scene
wolfing the macaronis
and I have read somewhere
the Meaning of Existence
yet have forgotten
just exactly where.
But I am the man
And I'll be there.
And I may cause the lips
of those who are asleep

to speak.
And I may make my notebooks
into sheaves of grass.
And I may write my own
eponymous epitaph
instructing the horsemen
to pass.

Vincent Ferrini

ELLIS ISLAND REDISCOVERED

the bird
the fish
FERRINI

on the graffiti wall
of the Examination Room
of Ellis Island
(the fish is drawn in blue chalk by
the health inspector)
1907
when my parents came over
on separate boats
in 3rd class steerage

the bird about to fly away to freedom here
with the fish

the Eye of the Pyramid
taking in the Pilgrims,

the Puritans,
the on coming immigrants

the foreign sounding minorities
becoming the majority
as we start again
with the solitaire

in the Church of the Fisherfolk

& I, in the languages of shoes & fishes

Diana Festa

Afterwards

La Dolce Vita –
there was a gilded Jesus swinging
from a helicopter over Roman roofs,
do you remember?
Images were packed with symbols,
the passionate pursuit of pleasure in sustained
images of decadence — dregs of a World War.

The statue hung on strings, swung
over roofs and terraces like a marionette,
in the deafening rumble of the helicopter.

There was that monster fish at the closing,
marooned on the beach,
one blank eye directed at us.
There was the Botticellian girl waving farewell
from beyond the dunes.

We wanted to hide as during the war,
hide reproach and pain, memories
of garroted childhood —
fire still burned within, fear still gripped
our fingers unhealed from digging
to disinter hope.

And in the quiet of a few rumbleless days,
we breathed in the open air.

More wars have followed.
Each time some plaster image dangles
at the edge of a past that sweeps over us
with the dead stare of a swollen fish.

Late in the day, I scrutinize the sky
for a sight of Minerva's owl
flying at dusk.

Jonathan Galassi

Morning Run

Villa Doria Pamphili, Rome

Often you start the day here, when the sun
is softest, having only just begun
climbing, and the lowest foliage steams,
clearing itself of nightsweat and the dreams
of the old city waking into heat,
crowdedness, poverty, terror, human dirt.
You dodge the lines of traffic where you can
and jog up a to a neoclassic span
of russet stucco crowned with limestone lords,
arms, and abbreviated Latin words
memorializing Innocent,
who "pamphilized" Rome, then past his monument
and under shade along an aqueduct
through which St. Peter's cupola — the top
alone — gleams like a gazebo or a teahouse
adrift in farmland, eloquent and senseless,
and veer left at a second, smaller gate
through undergrowth and past the headless late-
Imperial boy in an embarrassed pose
to come out on a scraggly field where rose,
bluebell and poppy manage to be seen
amid tall grass, no longer really green.

The orangery that brackets the Casino
is eerie, sun-dazed, bleached and empty now,
its maze of formal gardens gone to seed,
the terra-cotta tubs profuse with weed,
the walkways overrun, the statues down,
like the old town of tombs the house was built on
— and the façade, all filleting and frieze,
peeling and opulent in the thin haze.
Belrespiro, where the favored came
for respite from the heat and stench of Rome
to breathe free in a nature they could mold,
symmetrical, humane, rich and controlled,
all disappearing now in ripe confusion,
waste and disparity, the baroque tension
of topiary, marble, sky and trees
lost to corruption, disarray and ease.
Eight o'clock and there is just a breeze
stirring the tallest ilex, papal bees
are working in the flowers and the birds
are filling up the silence with their words.
The emptiness reverberates as air,
light, heat, scent, color, timelessness: desire.
You gather energy and take the stairs —
leftover heads and bodies everywhere —
three at a time to reach the fields the boys
will pepper later with their games and noise
and shirts and hair, as lover paired with lover
will lie down in the grove beyond and hover
between decorum and abandon, spread-
eagled together on the needle bed,

while down the hill the pensioners complain
over their *bocce* in the shady lane.
In a low wall you find another gate.
The fields beyond are wild, unmown, and yet
water is running in the knee-high straw,
fountains are playing somewhere, someone saw
an order here, too . . . and you make it out:
the lake below, its curve that swings about
halfway through the vista like a scythe
and finds its echo in the twining, lithe
limbs of Bernini's several mingled writhing
nymphs, who mock your fervor to embrace
the weather and the moment and the place.
You are alone here, yet you seem
verging on some encounter, some deep dream
surfacing in which the body tries
to become nature and the world complies —
a fusing with the air, a loss of self
into an energy that could be life,
a surging forward to become the wind,
hunger no experience can end
half satisfied in being body, sweat,
speed, color, an equivalence of heat,
while the repeating rhythm of your feet
synchs with your breathing till it is your heartbeat
and the land you're running on is ocean,
rising and falling, fluent with your motion
until you can believe you are the day,
you are the sun that brings life and decay,

that warms and soothes and in a moment turns
merciless and withers, burns.

You keep on running, closed inside your breath's
spondaic trance of oneness, power and health,
follow the ragged trees, as overgrown
as your own eagerness for the unknown
which threatens to spill forth at every turn
until you rise once more to a new plain,
another level, a new rush of pain,
and sprint down an aisle of poplars to a barn,
which was the goal.

And now you must return.
You round the mottled walls, the moment shifts,
the sunlight broadens and the last cloud lifts
over Monteverde, where the day
is gathering its errands. The caffès
are crowding and the gates are going up
over the shopfronts. Time to call a stop
to your exuberance, time to be tame and calm.
The morning's work is waiting in your room.
You leave the park to other runners now.
Trapped in their heavy clothes or else extreme
in their expertise, their search for form,
they seem to need to work against the heat,
but you for once luxuriate in sweat
as you lope halfway down the hill to home
and bath and coffee, and one look at Rome
from the window, laid out like a brain,

its crenelations steaming: your demesne,
or so it looks this morning, from this height —
who knows the colors it will wear tonight?
You gaze again, then shut away its din
and face the table, ready to begin.

Mary Giaimo

For Jessica, Between Continents

This pear is spun
of heat of your in-laws' bakery
and the ocher of its Renaissance street
the odor of bread rising,
your father-in-law's sweating cheeks
and the bile
that rings the iris of his hazel eyes.

A pear like this you split
into its two guitar halves
white flesh plucked
white flesh we took
with shavings of parmigiano
white fingers of your pale Tuscan husband
strumming the strings of a burnished guitar.
You carried us all captive to America, he thinks.
La donna sempre commanda, he said once to
me.

Here you still paint the old way
in tempera made with eggs
in oils and pine spirits
linen canvas primed in rabbit-skin glue
and whitewashed with floury gesso

while at the ovens in Florence your in-laws
wade through flour and heroin,
their boy Tiziano locked up in rehab.

The smell of a pear
was in the dragon faces of pale irises
growing wild along the empty lane in Greve,
that late-spring day you taught country mothers
and their kids to draw,
and I was loose on the road alone.
In an empty field I lay down,
pulled my shirt off to feel some kind of kiss
on my breasts, tall grass
and sun, insect legs and wind.
Waking, I rolled over to find a farmhand
watching me,
a stone's throw off,
black hair coiling close to his head,
Bacchus sweating at work
patiently coiling the vines
to stakes driven into the breast of the earth.
He turned around to piss
(Tuscan delicacy)
then turned back to me,
his purple cluster in his hand.

He smiled.
His vineyard knife hung at his belt.

Slowly I pulled my shirt on, packed my books,
walked to the road, slowly,
to belie him and the hissing
that no one knew where I was
no one knew who I was
but you.

David Giannini

DUSK

This is the light that makes the drivers imprecise and cats more arbitrary. This time of day, Jung knew, is the world's downcasting flight, when the black tribe people-of-the-dance-and-daylong-smile feel death, grow down into themselves as plants with no other way to reach, and the crow folds his sorrow in the neighboring limbs.

I move indoors; can't locate what's gone from me. It must be the light is going.

My body feels dark as its locked-in blood. It knows an unspeaking place, yet one sentence it must bear into the world: *What moves – moves through.*

I rise to switches, turn up dry ponds of light. Your presence is everywhere, sustaining what they cannot open. Everything not in them has your hair.

Sandra M. Gilbert

Mafioso

Frank Costello eating spaghetti in a cell at San Quentin,
Lucky Luciano mixing up a mess of bullets and
calling for parmesan cheese,
Al Capone baking a sawed-off shotgun into a
huge lasagna—
are you my uncles, my
only uncles?

O Mafiosi,
bad uncles of the barren
cliffs of Sicily—was it only you
that they transported in barrels
like pure olive oil
across the Atlantic?

Was it only you
who got out at Ellis Island with
black scarves on your heads and cheap cigars
and no English and a dozen children?

No carts were waiting, gallant with paint,
no little donkeys plumed like the dreams of peacocks.

Only the evil eyes of a thousand buildings
stared across at the echoing debarkation center,
making it seem so much smaller than a piazza,

only a half dozen Puritan millionaires stood on the wharf,
in the wind colder than the impossible snows of the Abruzzi,
ready with country clubs and dynamos

to grind the organs out of you.

Maria Mazziotti Gillan

LEARNING GRACE

"When you do something with your hands," my mother said, "you have to put your love into it, and then, it will be sacred. See?" She kneaded the bread dough, turned it over and over in her hands until her hands and the dough did their own special dance. Then she placed the dough back in its bowl, covered it with the bleached white kitchen towels she made, and left it to rise. When the towel was a hill curving high above the rim of the bowl, she lifted the dough onto the floured bread board, rolled it and shaped it into huge round loaves and long ones and, at Easter, she braided it into special shapes and baked whole eggs in it in set patterns she learned when she was a girl in San Mauro from her own mother. With the dough, she made crosses over the eggs and painted egg yolks over the surfaces of the loaves; then whispered a prayer over each and carefully slid them into the oven where they filled the house with the satisfying aroma of baking bread. When she took the loaves out of the oven, she smiled and broke off a piece of one loaf for us to eat with butter. Later, when she brought the bread to the table, it was a ceremony, the way she carried it in, holding a beautiful braided bread out to us, its surface glowing brown gold, the tender way she laid it in the center of the table, the way she made the sign of the cross over the loaf before she cut into it, this sustenance, this beauty, this grace she taught us to pass on.

Dana Gioia

The Lost Garden

If ever we see those gardens again,
The summer will be gone–at least our summer.
Some other mockingbird will concertize
Among the mulberries, and other vines
Will climb the high brick wall to disappear.

How many footpaths crossed the old estate–
The gracious acreage of a grander age–
So many trees to kiss or argue under.
And greenery enough for any mood.
What pleasure to be sad in such surroundings.

At least in retrospect. For even sorrow
Seems bearable when studied at a distance,
And if we speak of private suffering,
The pain becomes part of a well-turned tale
Describing someone else who shares our name.

Still, thinking of you, I sometimes play a game.
What if we had walked a different path one day.
Would some small incident have nudged us elsewhere
The way a pebble tossed into a brook
Might change the course a hundred miles downstream?

The trick is making memory a blessing,
To learn by loss the cool subtraction of desire,
Of wanting nothing more than what has been,
To know the past forever lost, yet seeing
Behind the wall a garden still in blossom.

John Giorno

La Saggezza Delle Streghe
(Wisdom of the Witches)

On a cold, early November night,
Mimmo, Martino, and I climbed to the top
of the Norman rock tower of Castelmezzano.
In the green lips of the trees,
the Dolomite mountain peaks of Basilicata,
big, broken splintered teeth spiked into the sky,
and a thin crescent moon.
Fog blew in from the blackness,
clouds rolled in below
and swirled around us,
and exposed briefly by a beam of light,
fled quickly, slipped back into the pitch black,
stumbled up and danced down the stone slopes,
and rushed in to touch, embrace and welcome us.

Hidden inside the fog and mists
were witches,
each a secret to herself,
the white witch with the curved knife and the bella figura,
the red witch made of ruby with a voluptuous body,
the blue witch with an owl face
rode a donkey with three legs,
the yellow witch wore a ball gown of gold brocade

and held a mongoose vomiting jewels,
the green witch with a hawk face rode a camel
and scorpions came from her fingertips,
and the beautiful witch with a smiling face
held a lamp of the sun and moon,
the witches of fog ate the witches of snow,
and witches dressed in black rode white dogs,
and danced, flew, chased, glided, and leaped over,
and long dives from life to death,
and witches who were rotting in hell
swarmed, screeching with joy.
They were happy to see us.

The witch Santa Meurte was a skeleton
with a grim-reaper sickle and a blood curdling grin.
She usually wore black,
but occasionally liked feather boas and sequin gowns,
and big fake jewels and necklaces,
and rings on each bone finger.
She chain smoked cigarettes and joints,
drank whiskey straight, and snorted drugs.
She had no flesh, but loved sex and bliss.
She danced exquisitely the criminal tango.
Santa Meurte answered the prayers of the poorest
and most outcast,
people in trouble adored her,
whores and drug dealers,
car thieves, burglars, and con-artists sought her protection,
people prayed for the miracle of money for food,

and the lost and abandoned.
Every single one who asked her help, she helped.
Santa Meurte was the wish-fulfilling witch.

The witch of poetry was Sarasvati
and her sister Laxmi was the witch of wealth.
When Sarasvati wrote great poems
and sang beautiful songs
and filled the world with music and wisdom,
and became famous and adored
for her brilliance, beauty, and compassion,
her sister Laxmi got very jealous, and angry,
and did the most terrible things.
She stole the cash and property,
lied, invented false gossip,
had her excluded,
and had the lawyers sue
blocking everything from happening;
she punished her for her success,
sweet revenge.
That is why poets never have money.
Poets are poor sisters,
with great clarity and great bliss.

Put your ear to stone
and open your heart to the sky,
put your ear to stone
and open your heart to the sky,
put your ear to stone

and open your heart to the sky,
put your ear to stone
and open your heart to the sky.

Ugly and beautiful witches,
peaceful and wrathful witches,
increasing and magnanimous witches,
are the outer displays of wisdom,
witches of water, witches of earth,
witches of fire, witches of air,
witches of space
are the inner wisdoms,
witches of fabulous sex in the union of great bliss
are the secret wisdoms,
and witches of great compassion and emptiness
are the innermost wisdoms.

Mimmo, Martino, and I climbed back down
the rocky mountain path,
as if feathers were under our feet,
and we walked down below the clouds,
on steps cut in the rock toward the medieval stone houses
that clung to the edge of the mountain peaks,
thousands of modulating waves of sweet sound
sang in silence.

Daniela Gioseffi

ORTA NOVA, *Provincia di Puglia*

"Land of bright sun and colors,"
you're called in *Italia.*
Near Bari and Brindisi where the ferry
has travelled the *Adriatico,*
to and from Greece for centuries.
Orta Nova, city of my dead father's birth.
How strange to view you, *piccolo villagio,*
with ladybugs, my talisman, landed on my shirt.

They show me your birth
certificate — "Donato Gioseffi, born 1905,"
scrawled in ink, on browning paper.
When I tell them I'm an author, first of my American family
to return to my father's home, I'm suddenly "royalty!"

They close the *Municipio* to take me in their best town car
to an archeological dig near the edge of the city.
There, the Kingdom of Herdonia, unearthed with its brick road
leading to Rome, as all roads did and still do,
back to antiquity's glory! Ladybugs rest on me at the dig
of stone sculptures the Belgian professor shows me. I buy his book,
"The Kingdom of Herdonia: Older Than Thebes."

Ah, *padre mio,* the taunts you took as a thin,
diminutive, "guinea" who spoke no English
in his fifth-grade class
from brash Americans of an infant country!

You never returned to your ancient land where now the natives,
simpatici pisani, wine and dine me in their best
ristorante. I insist on paying the bill. They give me jars
of *funghi* and *pimento* preserved in olive oil — their prize
produce to take back home with me. They nod knowingly,
when in talking of you, I must leave the table to weep —
alone in the restroom, looking into the mirror
at the eyes you gave me, the hands so like yours
that turn the brass faucet
and splash cold water over my face.
For an instant, in this foreign place, I have met you again,
Father, and have understood better, your labors,
your struggle, your pride, your humility,
the peasantry from which you came to cross the wide
sea, to make me a poet of New York City.
Which is truly my home?

This *piccolo villaggio* near Bari, with its old university,
the province where Saint Nicholas's Turkish bones are buried,
in hammered-gold and enameled reliquary,
the province of limestone caves full of paintings older than
those of Lescaux,

this white town of the Gargano, unspoiled by *turisti*, this land of color
sunlight and beauty. This home where you would have been happier
and better understood than in torturous Newark tenements of
your youth.
This land of sunlight, blue sky, pink and white flowers, white
stucco houses,
and poverty, *mezzogiorno*, this warmth you left to make me
a poet from New York City, indifferent place,
mixed of every race, so that I
am more cosmopolitan
than these, your villagers, or you
could ever dream of being.

This paradoxical journey
back to a lost generation
gone forever paving the way
into a New World
from the Old.

Arturo Giovannitti

The Bum

The dust of a thousand roads, the grease
And grime of slums, were on his face;
The fangs of hunger and disease
Upon his throat had left their trace,
The smell of death was in his breath,
But in his eye no resting place.

Along the gutters, shapeless, fagged,
With drooping head and bleeding feet,
Throughout the Christmas night he dragged
His care, his woe, and his defeat;
Till gasping hard with face downward
He fell upon the trafficked street.

The midnight revelry aloud
Cried out its glut of wine and lust;
The happy, clean, indifferent crowd
Passed him in anger and disgust;
For — fit or rum — he was a bum,
And if he died 'twas nothing lost.

The tramp, the thief, the drunk, the brute,
The beggar, each withdrew his eye;
E'en she, the bartered prostitute,

Held close her skirts and passed him by;
For, drunk or dead, the street's the bed
Where dogs and bums must sleep and die.

So all went on to their debauch,
Parade of ghosts in weird array.
Only a tramp dog did approach
That mass of horror and decay —
It sniffed him out with its black snout
Then turned about and limped away.

And there he lay, a thing of dread,
A loathsome thing for man and beast;
None put a stone beneath his head,
Or wet his lips, or rubbed his wrist,
And none drew near to help or cheer —
Save a policeman and a priest.

Yet neither heard his piteous wail,
And neither knelt by where he fell.
The man in blue spoke of the jail,
Until he heard his rattle tell,
And hearing that, he motioned at
The man in black to speak of hell.

To speak of hell, lest he should hope
For peace, for rest untroubled, deep,
Where he no more need roam and grope
Through dark, foul lanes to beg and weep,

Where in the vast warm earth at last
He'd find a resting place to sleep.

To sleep — not standing tired and sick
By grimy walls and cold lamp poles,
Nor crouched in fear of the night stick,
To beat his sore and swollen soles,
Nor see the flares of green nightmares
And ghastly dawns through black rat holes;

To sleep beneath the green, warm earth
As in a sacred mother's womb,
And wait the call of a new birth,
When his dead life again shall bloom —
For it shall pass into the grass;
The lamb will graze upon his tomb.

Not he, not he shall think of this,
Not he the wretched, the down trod;
Beyond the club of the police
Shall reach the ruthless hand of God,
For like a ghoul the rich man's rule
Will seek him out beneath the sod.

He must know hell, lest he should guess
That all his weary tramp is o'er —
A hell of hunger and distress
Where he, cold, naked and footsore,

Alone and ill, must wander still
Through endless roads forevermore.

Nay, nay, my brother, 'tis a lie!
Just like their Christ, their love, their law!
They brewed a wolfish fiend on high,
Just like their hearts perverse and raw,
To damn or save the dying slave,
So those who live should serve in awe.

So that in trembling fear they'd hold
Upon their neck their masters' sway,
So that they'd guard their masters' gold
And starve and freeze and still obey,
So when for greed they toil and bleed,
Instead of rising they should pray.

That's why they come to huts and slums!
'Tis not to soothe or to console,
But just to stay the hungry bums
With this black terror of the soul,
And bend and blight with chains of fright
What chains of steel could not control.

And yet, and yet the thunderbolt
Shall fall some day they fear the least,
When flesh and sinews shall revolt
And she, the mob, the fiend, the beast,
Unchained, awake, shall turn and break
The bloody tables of their feast.

But you, my brother, will be dead,
And none will think of you for aye!
Still by your spirit I'll be led,
If like their cattle you'll not die,
If you'll but show before you go
That mine can be your battle cry!

Aye, brother, death all woes relieves —
Yet this low world that well you knew,
This Christian world of sainted thieves
And fat apostles of virtue,
This world of brutes and prostitutes,
Must see its end revealed by you!

Rise then! Your rags, your bleeding shirt,
Tear from your crushed and trampled chest,
Fling in its face its own vile dirt,
Your scorn and hate to manifest,
And in its gray cold eyes of prey
Spit out your life and your protest!

Peter Gizzi

Wintry Mix

The 6 A.M. January
encaustic clouds
are built
in a waxy gray putty
whizzing by with spots
of luminous silver
crack-o'-the-world light
coming through, an eerie
end-o'-the-world feeling
yet reassuring
like an old movie.
Do I really have to go out there?
Now a hint of muted
salmon tones breaking
a warmish band
of welcoming pinkish light.
Is it like this every morning?
My head still in the dark.
Worry, eck! But the brightening
russet tipped cloud ballet
reminds me of something
in Pliny, yea, Pliny.
Can't imagine opening
the door today in a toga.

Work and more,
yes, work
sends us into the draft.

Rose Basile Green

FOURTEENTH SUNDAY AFTER PENTECOST

You say that I two masters may not serve,
For each would claim my incense and my hand;
That in dividing parts of my preserve
In two, one would the other reprimand.
The lily needs no cloth to bear the sun
While I hug gilded garments in the snow.
The birds don't harvest, for the seeds they shun,
That I have planted, but the crop must grow.
The poor in hungry toil dream not of wine,
For when they breathe those fumes, their substance dies;
And wine alone cannot delight the soul,
For bread must line the cup wherein it lies.

But, why, if I revere you with the perfume of the rose,
May I not prime the soil that bleeds the color where it blows?

George Guida

The Italian American Satan

Thirty-three years old,
I refuse to father my parents' *nipoti.*

Once, at a Christmas family dinner,
I renounced my interest in Italian women.
Not my type, I declared,
turning from the table.

Intelligent, suburban, well-fed,
I have pursued
neither business, nor law, nor medicine.

One lazy Sunday morning,
I took a mailed photograph
of my second cousin's newborn
and threw it in the trash.

On the eve of my year in Italy,
I dressed up as the Pope
and had sex with my Jewish girlfriend.

Locked in my rootless room,
I spill my family's guts on paper,
overwhelming *omertá.*

And for this, other demons praise me.

Gerry LaFemina

FREIGHT

At night I hear the clacking of trains; I hear them stop outside of town, & the echoing crash of train cars being joined reverberates over my neighborhood's roofs. It reminds me of billiard balls coming together on the green fields of my youth. How I'd cut class for nine ball & how then the kiss of those balls reminded me of bodies, of lips, of the girls I knew & never knew & wish I knew better. What I thought was intimacy. & the men there: old Luigi & Howie the Hat (because of that rain-stained fedora he always wore) – they held my hand over the cue & taught me how to bridge. Howie would talk about the trains he rode during the depression: they took him away from that city & brought him back years later, the streets still cobblestoned, all the storefronts changed. There are nights when I walk into Spike's Keg of Nails right by the train tracks & listen & place four quarters into the bar table for fifteen balls. I'll stand there, those colorful globes spinning & moving by trajectories few understand, & I'll hold a cue gently, the way I was taught, thinking to myself: rhythm: stroke & follow through.

Teresa Leo

P.S.

The end is not near. We've passed the end, and it's so far back
it's like the tit of a cow in a field of poppies, a dot in a field

of many dots in a painting a myopic man is straining to see
in a village museum near a city we've never been to

nor will. It's so far back I can't remember the exact
moment of it, the way I didn't see the curve ball coming,

the one that clipped my left hip as I swung the bat,
missing and not being missed. It's the part of the eraser

worn down to the black metal band, the one that left
hideous gashes in the page of the test the math teacher

sprung on us, so many equations without solutions,
numbers that divided like soldiers on a reconnaissance mission,

then divided again. It's in the back of the closet
in the box of Thank You cards I put stamps on

and never sent. It's that last conversation,
the staccato of conjunctions that kept each noun at bay,

the one that wound down to the luxury of nonspecifics —
the possibility of *or*, the horror of *but*, the delusion of *and.*

It passed me by, the way beauty, like disease,
has been known to skip a generation.

P. H. Liotta

The Blue Whale

Drifting on a river she could not control, the broken carcass of a blue whale came to our shores. By then, jaw already cracked from the prop-blade of a ship, she lingered too long at the surface, unable to feed. Struck by a tanker crossing from Anvers to Providence, buoyed by the bulbous chin of the bow, the leviathan never knew what hit her. Water pressure kept the corpse in place until they entered Narragansett Bay. Dead a week already, she was gaffed and hooked and dragged alongside the pilot boat to Second's Beach.

Back then, no one knew if she were male or female. "She" could glory in the sand while "he" grew fetid and fell away, waiting for dissection. The skeleton would be buried in the dunes, in secret, when it was done. Like the odd doctor in Marlow's darkness, who measures the crania of those who drift "out there" and "up the Congo," with caliper-like things, "in the interest of science." *Oh, I never see them come back,* he said.

By the time I get there, cubism has set in. A thousand faces circle the cadaver. The dead remains: a wishbone bent toward nothing, inverted jawbone jabs at sky. Mist fizzles into rain. The organs splayed out in the drift sizzle like the sound of crackling bacon. Each fleck of water slices at the desiccated blood. There's still enough to feel the loss. A river of baleen. A disembodied fluke.

Two days on, the ebb of human flotsam has washed clean. "He" and "she" are going now-into the gloam. A bulldozer grumbles in the downpour: a single beacon, tachistoscopic, flaming red. And when the three of us arrive, everyone and thing are gone. My daughter turns in wind and keeps on asking, *What did she look like? Why did she die?* Just face the sea, the pictures of a floating world: the subject sees but never speaks. The way you fear the menace left unsaid–the natural convergence weighing down. You dream alone.

Out there, what difference between what stretches ahead and what is past? The Acropolis and Parthenon, streaming into view. The ruined Balkans, hope and slaughter. Breadlines in St. Petersburg.

Kurds fleeing from the bombing runs. Head for the Kyrgiz steppe. See for yourself: the free spillage of Tajik blood or the chaos-order of the Taliban. The black sturgeon, up from Caspian depths, flashing through air. Behold the nothing that is not there and the nothing that is.

I don't know about you. But for me, we're drifting still. I see the wreck of a whale, watch it going, going . . . like seals in the outer harbor, who tumble in brine and do their best ignoring death, like the one tied to the mast with wax in ears who was forced not to listen, what good could come in reading the runes of a ruined life? O lantern without bearer, you, too, are drifting to spite your course. And the earth was salt before the ocean turned to tears.

Gian Lombardo

FIELD OF VIEW

To what hold the candle? In this obscure light, every shadow betrays the passing of a possible villain.

Flame flickers in the breath of nefarious laughter. Against walls vagrant penumbrae make sure the joke gets you. Never the other way round.

Once eyes foreclose on following faint shifts, piles of wax enter dreams.

No matter how many times, no matter how hard the try, the drop cannot be run back up the shaft.

Matt Longabucco

These My Exhortations

If I had the wherewithal, I would burn the notebook
in which I scribble images — city, river, sky —
ominous only to an ominous mind.

Ambiguity, I detest you! Your simultaneity is a fraud;
you require two or more moments to exist,
and then you make us the dupes of Time, and we put
our tongue to the diode to suck the weak pitiful sensation,
like eating a particular food once too often in a week
or coming for the third time in a day.

I'd like a giant typewriter, whose every key, when struck,
would leave by its one mechanical swat an entire poem
on the page. Then what prepositions, what predicates, even,
I could offer you; failing which, I'd be an enormous fly
in the lands of sugar cane.

Alessandra Lynch

Carousel

The brutal white horses with painted-on faces
Are riding their circles, riding
Dead air. The dead air is hanging,
Is ridden with riders and glued-on red
Saddles. Crumpled hoofs in the dead-on air.

The wild glare of the brutal white horses
And the crippled gold manes tossing
Dead air and the two girls who ride them throwing
Their kisses from high, battered foreheads
Through the thin screams of their stringy red hair.

The brutal white horses are riding their circles,
Veering in terror from painted-on ropes
In dead-earnest air. The ropes that suspend them.
The brutal flare of their painted-in nostrils, the brutal
Whirl of their unfurling manes in the painted-on air.

Their paralyzed mouths the yellow bit snares,
Their petrified stares tapped by flies riding air
And they're riding in silence, glassed in
By air and the two girls who poke them
Dead in the eye and pound their fists on
The painted-on flanks are beginning to cry.

For the brutal white horses don't bolt or whinny, don't
Ever die, but ride their dead circles, noses on high,
The dead air upon them, the painted-on saddles
And painted-on reins, and painted-on lives. What mind
Would have them, circling and glassy, immune
And frozen in constant alarm.

Anne Marie Macari

Annunciation

When I asked her how the world began
my mother's face went blank.

I was very young, trying for the first time
to see the universe as endless.

All I saw was darkness swirling into itself.
How could anything be endless?

But how could it be contained? By what? All cosmos
held in the crook of an elbow?

There were no answers, though I thought the clouds
were great wings trying

to help me, and thought my blood changed
directions. What could I be

but an echo? Stranded here while the universe
grows like a belly dense

with stars. And I thought we were all orbiting inside
that belly, and light could pass

through me but I wouldn't feel it. Years later,
my son told me how

he was conceived. He said he stood in a cloud
and pointed at me: *I want her*,

then put down his bow and arrow and came
when my back was turned

and entered through my shoulder blades.
What I don't know

is everything: stars, sand, salt, dust,
molecules and atoms,

and how they come scudding through the door
full of news from distances

I can't imagine. Someday I'll tell my sons
the truth, that I knew

they were coming. Nothing I could see or even
feel but a sense sometimes

that I was permeable, the cells inside me
gathering and spreading.

I hate to think of galaxy after galaxy. All matter
burning up and shucked off.

The endless signs of demise and change.
I still can't grasp

how anything at all can exist and what made
the maker. And sometimes I'm choked

with love and forget my own ignorance.
Maybe just at that moment

light is pressing through a tree and reaching
my window, and I am

satisfied, joyful, though I know there's
nothing there, just light,

announcing itself, coming through.

Gerard Malanga

GIORGIO MORANDI

Morandi's name disappears among the concrete chicanes,
the weathervanes nervous and grieving
the whispering elms with their ghostly demeanor, their tips swaying
or the hand without trumps or the brush that goes with it

and then suddenly it doesn't. Or off in the distance
surf pounding the shore along the Costa Leuca
not the view from his 4 storey window,
not your 5 o'clock shadow, not the dog days of August
but almost. And then the name remains hidden awhile
or the street or the tram tracks go sleeping,
or as if several blue jays were pretending a rout
then turned around causing much mischief.
The petals the stamens the meagre corollas tangled and drooping.
The table askew. A thick gloom descending.

Sarah Manguso

EVERYTHING

Before I gave my eyes to a liar with ruined entrails
I saw the shape for the fifteenth time.

I thought I saw how the story got told.
And I gave it everything.

Blind I listen to all the little sounds.
How pretty they are.
I arrive and arrive.
Look — I am the statue that thinks it's running.

Mary Ann Mannino

LEAF LEAVING

The leaf, defiant yellow, in the grass
— risk taker —
let go, floated down.
In another glowing gold autumn
God packs things up.
Cleans house.
Tosses the out-of-date
Gets ready for winter's
wash down.

Like me
leaving
my yesterdays
hoarded in smoke-stained boxes
in the attic of my house.
What should I do with my first communion dress?
The cancelled checks of thirty years, recording the prices
of nursery school, the new kitchen, the divorce?
My father's last coat? — I see him wearing it "dressed-up"
for a funeral, a Christmas visit, to see a school play.
Or the sweater my mom was knitting when she died?
It was for me — a bottle green — the needles still in it
just like she left them.
Or the top of my wedding cake—bride and groom under a
wedding bell, still young and smiling?

My ex-husband's baby shoes, my mother-in-law's deep fryer,
My father-in-law's high school sweater — blue with a white
Football letter.
The weight of so many lives.
My dead brother's trains, the lead soldiers he made while sick

Do I dare
Like the leaf
Let go and in
One glorious adventure
Float lighter than air
Across the driveway
Down the block
Further?

Paul Mariani

The Old Men Are Dying

After the three days' watch, after the flowers
are tossed into a heap, after the last mourner,
feeling the coming on of the autumn squall, turns
and leaves, the crew comes to seal the boxes, caulking them,

screwing the tops down tight, to make them seaworthy
for the last long voyage. The little boats tug
against their moorings until they pull free at last
and begin moving toward the north, a north

more north than any the dead pilots have ever
sailed before. Two uncles gone in three short
months. How the four remaining brothers huddle
closer now for warmth against the coming cold.

Twice my brother and myself had to make the trip
south from western Massachusetts to New York to pay
our last respects. And what was there to say? That
the old men were dying? First Victor, my father's

dead sister's husband. Short-order cook and journeyman
mechanic, his family from Milan. Bertazzo lopped
to Bert. Strokes broke him until he listed badly.
One more and I will not come back, he said, and meant it.

When that one hit him, he turned to face the wall,
turned north those last six weeks, until the dark snows
swept him up and he was gone, without a word, the way he was
in life. Then John, the burly one, his whole life lived

on the same mean street. Mayor of Sixty-first
and First, the neighbors came to call him, as his
Little Italy turned to swinging singles' paradise
around him. In the old photos I can see how strong

he must have been, so that I do not doubt the tales
my father told me of his brother and, for what
they're worth, I have passed on to my sons. How
he pinned two men to a barroom table by their throats,

one with his huge left paw, one with his right. How
for years he lifted kegs of prohibition booze
and lugged ice boxes five flights down to the old Ford
van. How he raised the back end of a Packard

while a buddy fixed a flat. It ate him slow, the cancer,
ate his stomach first, then the rest. Leaving
his last room late, I walked down five flights
of empty waking rooms, saw the unattended open coffins,

each with its still pilot waiting to set sail north.
And what was there to say? All sorts were there
to bid their last goodbyes: those who'd made their mark
and those who'd missed. With the greatgrandchildren

all family looks are lost. The blood gets too thinned out,
the young enter a world we never knew. Julia
and Giuseppi: left Compiano some ninety years ago.
Settled in New York with a million others like them.

Their first: run down outside their flat at sixteen
by a drunken iceman who jumped the curb and splattered him.
Siciliano, those from the north of Italy shrugged,
then turned away. For what was there to do? Once

my father sat on his sister's pineslab coffin, roped
to the flat back of the horsedrawn wagon as his family
began the long procession across the 59th Street bridge,
headed for Calvary. Too young then to understand,

he smiled into the camera. Now even he must feel
the cold. You see it when the four brothers gather
at family picnics, then turn, each one alone, to watch
the ducks drifting in the stagnant pond. They stare

at the water in the last light of Long Island summer
and, though they never talk of it, brace themselves
for the time when their little boats will be cut
loose and, dressed in their best navyblue two-piece suits,

their leathery browned hands folded stiffly
right over left with the polished black beads
between them, they begin to drift out through the once
familiar channels for the last trip north.

Donna Masini

GETTING OUT OF WHERE WE CAME FROM

I was born in Brooklyn.
Even the birds were dingy
and the dark courtyard between
buildings filled with grimy light
like the lit up inside of a pumpkin.
There we could be frantic.
There we could stamp and spin and
fall down pretending to be dead. Still
it is the place my father loves.
I see him slicing meats, stampeding streets —
wild teenage goodboy crowds
so near to me, on the lip of my dream
green workclothes still oil the air
of my bedroom, saturate the walls.
He works hard for you seven days a week.
In 1963, grease-soaked, shadowed
we ferried the harbor to a new home.
Barbecues. Mortgages. Assassinations.
The bridge went up. The basement flooded.
Up to our knees in water we bailed and bailed.
In their yards our neighbors laughed and drank
and shook their heads, *Too bad*
they didn't know the house was built on swamp.

Carole Maso

You Were Dazzle

What filled us those nights next to the ocean beside sorrow,
besides rage, besides pain was —

We were sadness and rage and pain, but we were —

phosphorescence —

the slam of the ocean

iridescent

You were gorgeous,

You were wild,

And how at night we listened to the water raging and stars.
I have not forgotten

glowing flowers in a barrel
flowers filling the room and dazzle

A summer afternoon. Your designer shoes and maids. Your Henry James. You could have anything, buy anything you wanted, you said:

"on your stomach this time"

crawling together, making something monstrous, through the sand.

In the ditch we were digging

or on the broken pier when you were slumming

those lustrous afternoons . . .

"guide me like a Carmelite . . ."

What filled us was rage and sorrow and hurt
The black veil of August descending and birds. Caught.
Trapped in the end. There's no way for this to work . . .

make me shudder once more

squirming under you

When you bit my lip it bled
    "go ahead."
salt and ocean and blood mixing
all the fluids of our bodies mixing
    and language

And you whisper "beg." And you whisper "fetch."

We were careless, we were sensational sex, the slam of the ocean — hallucinations:

On the beach at twilight materialized ten lifeguards to make a pyramid — I have not forgotten

The planks giving way,

The carelessness of our inflations: the pier suddenly on fire.

I wanted others and you were furious. I wanted others and you were humiliated.

The triangles you tried to negotiate.
the pyramids . . .
On a beach at dusk
we watched.

The fluorescent. Luminescent.

Humiliated you wanted to leave me before I left you. But you were sex addicted, addicted to our bodies together. And so you kept putting it off. Angrily. Growing to despise us both.

But I would never have left you.

Our sad history. I would never have left you.

We were alive —

The phosphorescent tide.
We were gorgeous and gleaming. Ecstatic.

Ride me like a saint. Guide me like a Carmelite.

We were tangle and pull and gag but we were dazzle.
We were hurt and heartbreak and never again —

We were strung out. We were strung up.

We were head pulled back and gleaming.
We were danger. We were ruin. We were
gasping and swoon. Abandon.

    "Go ahead"
You took off my suit
bit my nipples until —
left me naked.
a small tuft — scratchy then
    "go ahead"

You could have anything you wanted.
    "beg"

You were money and sensational sex in the blaring
afternoons.

You were rage, you were beauty, you were electric and what filled
us was light, what filled us was being completely alive.

phosphorescence

You who idolize power
                force
                lucidity
                definition
                rhapsodize   control
You were pompous
        grandiose
        pretentious
        competitive

I was danger, disorder.

A broken pier.

You said him or me.
Her or me.
Them or me.

I was hair pulled back.

The planks giving way under our weight, our glowing bones, your designer combat boots, your rage.

You were the consummate, you were the notorious: party girl, networker, careerist par excellence.

You were John Cheever and Henry James and Bridgehampton and rules and regulations.

We were losing our way.
You who commemorate "found" with flags,
"there," "home," with little stickers, markers,
medals, with rewards . . . You were losing your way and you were furious.

Kiss my clavicle.

We were flowers in a barrel (it took years to end) but we were dazzle.

Unending well of tears

We were always changing shape, a broken pier, flowers in a barrel, flames.

We were losing our way

you who idolize strength, definition, distance and I, source of disorder, random, falling, pressed close up

"God you are gorgeous."

We were doomed but we were unstoppable dazzle.

We were lost.
We were losing.
We were the memory of survive.

Tripping down the wayward aisle. The wooden planks giving up, giving way. A hand pinned back, forbidden.

And you whisper, "good girl's knot."

We were losing our way.

And you whisper, "beg."

exquisite hour

And you kiss my clavicle once more.

We were broken and fractured and fallen into water
refracted in light — shackled
Left for dead devoured by brightness — blinded

The memory of survive. I would never have left you.
Flowers in a barrel —

We were gorgeous on that dazzling and disappearing pier we were broken, fractured, fallen into water refracted in light and sadness—dazzle — it took years to end

And tangle and pull and regret

The phosphorescent tide don't go don't end
We were strung out   We were strung up

And you whisper "don't." And you whisper "go."

We were careless, we were sensational sex, the slam of the ocean —
hallucinations:

Ride me like a saint. (Guide me like a Carmelite.)

We were tangle and pull and gag but we were dazzle.
We were hurt and heartbreak and never again

Unending well of tears

We were always changing shape, a broken pier, flowers in a
barrel, flames

We were shipwrecked   we were reckless   we were wrecked

We were pull and regret.

We were too careless.   And too careful.

We were flagrant and we were rage. Conflagration: the pier suddenly on fire. Cremations. We were ashes. We were the memory of flowers in a barrel.

You who idolize power, money, force, definition, lucidity,
control

We were lost, we were losing. We were flower petals
floating in a barrel.
We were unstoppable dazzle.

We had lost our way and flames and flowers and always

changing shape.

You were flagrant, you were fury, you were fear. You were
decorum and rules and all of it doomed. You were broken
hearted and pier on fire

You were never again

And you were dazzle.

Stephen Massimilla

Clairvoyante

To the tinkle of domestic pianos
all afternoon up the street, leaves
were whispering as if they had a secret
but were afraid to interrupt.
Two, three birds on a wire, and none.

In the dim-lit back of a shop
with no sign, she'd heard human noise
through the wall, a closing door,
a cough. In a feathered shadow
with openings for eye and mouth only,

she fixed on a piece of sun quivering
under the shade. She was blind,
but, did her lips tremble? Dust
from old gems weighted down the drawers.
Clock talking to a clock.

Finally I had to look: the street
was completely gated up. Just a man
lying on the pavement with newsprint
over him. Fat feet stuck out.
One gypsy bird in the sky.

Jerome Mazzaro

LIBRARY TAPESTRY

That threaded brilliance, Hannibal in silk
gaping the elephants and fat as grouse,
his faded flesh the color of whole milk
against an armor's faded, silvery blues,
preserves the man as he was pictured once:
He stands among six well-groomed elephants,
plotting a final march on frightened Rome,
perfect except for stains left by the years,
which even careful cleanings cannot dim,
weaving a second tale upon his first.
One stain, the faded yellow of beef broth,
suspends his middle. I watch the tapestry,
my mother reading Invernizio
aloud, and think the stain some blood, for she
has told me blood stains fade a yellow.
Perhaps some prince was knifed against the cloth
as in her books? Savonarola waged
his war with Rome and pillaged Florence both
its art and men after the weaver staged
this scene; his heresy might cause such stains.
Or old Lorenzo, vomiting his pains,
dying, refusing finally to give in
to that disloyal monk he'd valued once,
deprived at last of his last absolution,
resting where his sleep's sweeter than a stone's.

Her voice absorbs. Caught in its dulling rounds
of family feuds and deadly treacheries,
I fight my boyish mind for English sounds,
staring beyond our arbor at the trees
that weave the borders of her Roman world
until I'm drowsed like Florence going mad,
or Hannibal among his milling herd,
waging a future, harmless, reckless raid
like Charles against a Vatican Swiss Guard,
staining my war with drops of lemonade.

Albert Mobilio

Pilgrims

In this they lived and lived almost
all of their years in this,
this house which is really a road
on which weather alights

At first there was something and
then there was less and then even
less and their leftover fruit sat out
and spoiled in the day's own sun

From this they left as if almost alive,
all of their tears on this,
this road that was never a house
on which weather alights

At last there was nothing and
then there was nothing else and then
only their own fruitless days which
spoiled and burst in the leftover sun

Stephen Murabito

Ethnic Poem
"In Memory of My Grandparents"

Here it comes
Through ruby glints
Of Uncle Leo's Chianti
And across the airspace
Inside this burning skull:
Bodies ascending stony Sicilian hillsides,
Spirits abundant as Catanian holy parades,
It's a flight, a flight: All of the lost relatives
Rise from the dead and surge now to the new world.
They are the songs of *pane*, Asiago, and olives on my breath!

Their hands shake, passion itself resurrecting their flesh.
They breathe Vivaldi through their eyes, exhale Dante in my ears.

And their children squirm with the small fires in their souls.
They're being held and told, *Hush, hush. Stay close, stay close.*
It's time now. We are returning, returning to his aching heart.

They want to cook and live and eat with their new friends;
They want to fill our faces with the blood of their smiles;
They want to touch us through the sauce and Romano we twirl
And twirl into yet another explosive dinner-table story.
Oh, let the world end; it'll begin again in breaths sweet as this
As they pass their lives into our veins, defy death, and sing,

Everyone, everyone, it's ready: Come, sit, eat, eat, eat!

Michael Palma

The Patron Saint of California

The patron saint of California
Wears both of his eyes
On one side of his face.
His head is long and curved,
Tilted to one side.
His nose points inward.
His face is turned
Westward, toward
The vast and cloudless sea.

He stands at the summit
Of a plump mountain
And whispers to the valley.
When the townsmen hear
His low, harsh croon
They put down their cabbages
And walk together, arms
Linked, laughing
And singing, down to the sea.

Michael Palmer

NOTES FOR ECHO LAKE 1

"I am glad to see you Ion."

He says this red as dust, eyes a literal self among selves and picks the coffee up.

Memory is kind, a kindness, a kind unlistening, a grey wall even toward which you move.

It was the woman beside him who remarked that he never looked anyone in the eye. (This by water's edge.)

This by water's edge.

And all of the song 'divided into silences', or 'quartered in three silences'.

Dear Charles, I began again and again to work, always with no confidence as Melville might explain. Might complain.

A message possibly intercepted, possibly never written. A letter she had sent him.

But what had his phrase been exactly, "Welcome to the Valley of Tears," or maybe "Valley of Sorrows." At least one did feel welcome, wherever it was.

A kind of straight grey wall beside which they walk, she the older by a dozen years, he carefully unlistening.

Such as words are. A tape for example a friend had assembled containing readings by H.D., Stein, Williams, others. Then crossing the bridge to visit Zukofsky, snow lightly falling.

Breaking like glass Tom had said and the woman from the island. Regaining consciousness he saw first stars then a face leaning over him and heard the concerned voice, "Hey baby you almost got *too* high."

Was was and is. In the story the subject disappears.

They had agreed that the sign was particular precisely because arbitrary and that it included the potential for (carried the sign of) its own dissolution, and that there was a micro-syntax below the order of the sentence and even of the word, and that in the story the subject disappears it never disappears. 1963: only one of the two had the gift of memory.

Equally one could think of a larger syntax, e.g. the word-as-book proposing always the book-as-word. And of course still larger.

Beginning and ending. As a work begins and ends itself or begins and rebegins or starts and stops. Ideas as elements of the working not as propositions of a work, even in a propositional art. (Someone said someone thought.)

That is, snow

a) is

b) is not

falling — check neither or both.

If one lives in it. 'Local' and 'specific' and so on finally seeming less interesting than the 'particular' wherever that may locate.

"What I really want to show here is that it is not at all clear *a priori* which are the simple colour concepts."

Sign that empties itself at each instance of meaning, and how else to reinvent attention.

Sign that empties . . . That is *he* would ask *her*. He would be the asker and she unlistening, nameless mountains in the background partly hidden by cloud.

The dust of course might equally be grey, the wall red, our memories perfectly accurate. A forest empty of trees, city with no streets, a man having swallowed his tongue. As there is no 'structure' to the sentence and no boundary or edge to the field in question. As there is every where no language.

As I began again and again, and each beginning identical with the next, meaning each one accurate, each a projection, each a head bending over the motionless form.

And he sees himself now as the one motionless on the ground, now as the one bending over. Lying in an alley between a house and a fence (space barely wide enough for a body), opening his eyes he saw stars and heard white noise followed in time by a face and a single voice.

Now rain is falling against the south side of the house but not the north where she stands before a mirror.

"Don't worry about it, he's already dead."

"Te dérange pas, il est déjà mort."

"È morto lei, non ti disturba."

She stands before the mirror touches the floor. Language reaches for the talk as someone falls. A dead language opens and opens one door.

So here is color. Here is a color darkening or color here is a darkening. Here white remains . . .

And you indicate the iris of the portrait's eye, a specific point on the iris, wanting that color as your own. There is a grey wall past which we walk arm in arm, fools if we do greater fools if we don't.

And I paint the view from my left eye, from the balcony of the eye overlooking a body of water, an inland sea possibly, possibly a man-made lake.

And do I continue as the light changes and fades, eventually painting in pitch dark. That is, if you write it has it happened twice

It rained again that night deep inside
where only recently had occurred the abandonment of signs

Joseph Papaleo

History Lesson For Friday

The Puerto Rican girls are blonde already,
having given up their darkness of good frescoes
to look like what they were told they should
to get ahead, avoid being overlooked.

This now leaves the Peruvians, Chileans, Koreans,
Salvadorans, Dominicans, Vietnamese, Jordanians,
Pakistani, Egyptians still in their natural colors
and styles because they do not know yet
that Marilyn came out of the bowels
of Jean Harlow for them.

But soon they will seek salvation
with yellow rinse
and try to become tall and pale and titless:
and if they succeed they lose their bodies,
and if they succeed they lose their souls.

Jay Parini

GRANDMOTHER IN HEAVEN

In a plume-field, white above the blue,
she's pulling up a hoard of rootcrops
planted in a former life and left to ripen:
soft gold carrots, beets, bright gourds.
There's coffee in the wind, tobacco smoke
and garlic, olive oil and lemon.
Fires burn coolly through the day,
the water boils at zero heat.
It's always almost time for Sunday dinner,
with the boys all home: dark Nello,
who became his cancer and refused to breathe;
her little Gino, who went down the mines
and whom they had to dig all week to find;
that willow, Tony, who became so thin
he blew away; then Julius and Leo,
who survived the others by their wits alone
but found no reason, after all was said,
for hanging on. They'll take their places
in the sun today at her high table,
as the antique beams light up the plates,
the faces that have lately come to shine.

Lucia Perillo

Lament in Good Weather

So would this be how I'd remember my hands
(given the future's collapsing trellis):
pulling a weed (of all possible gestures),
trespassing the shade between toppled stalks?
A whole afternoon I spent chopping them back, no fruit
but a glut of yellow buds, the crop choked
this year by its own abundance, the cages
overrun. And me now fond of tomatoes, really,
something about how when you cut to their hearts
what you find is only a wetness and seeds,
wetness and seeds, wetness and seeds.
Still, my hands came gloved with their odor
into his room, where for days I've searched
but found no words to fit.
Bitter musky acrid stale — the scent
of hands once buried past the wrist in vines.

Anthony Piccione

Napping Outside

It is the last of summer.
Light hums between the sunflowers
and our frog pond.
What did we dream of?

Nick Piombino

The Chase

The poet
alone with life
as day fades out
inhales the ellipsis
wish and dream
truth and desire
unnamed beads
on a chain

The sacrifice
once made, the
ear tells it
again from the
beginning
doubts surround
hopes, a logical
helix

No more imaginary
than real, invisible
exchanges mark a
phase of separation
and restraint, thoughts

occluded from
experience, nets
mistaken for touch

Regrets truncate
misfortunes, sounds
repeat the origins
which produced them
assent disguised as
resistance, a smile
on the face of
satisfaction

Opposite realities
dissolve inside and
pose themselves as doubles,
as choices

as words attempt
to hide from their own
effigies, blend into
themselves and
disappear

Frank Polite

The Last Part Of The Interview

. . . and what have you decided
to do now?

To leave.

Where will you go?
Are you well enough to travel?

Well enough.

Do you plan to travel with someone
or alone?

Alone.

One last question, if you don't mind.
What, finally, has come through
to you? I mean, after all these years
what have you learned?

To leave, well enough, alone.

Lia Purpura

Though I Am Not

Though I am not Catholic I know
today is scented like a censer,
that a censer imitates cut-pine air,
the raw stump itself is the face of the moon,
and dark is what every day turns to.

And though I do not sit, contemplative, for long
before an idea about darkness comes,
I arrest it and keep it a few steps in front of me,
turned just so, as the deer turned one afternoon
that I might observe how ribs taper to a soft spot
before the haunch starts, how slack it goes there
and dim where the hide folds tenderly down the bone.
I might have seen where a bullet goes
but I made of that place a darkened window,
which is, of course, a mirror.

And though I am not the object its heart wants,
I know the brute machinery a hummingbird can be,
that it idles at the open hand of the blown rose,
and from that softened, debilitated pool
sips of the sweetest irony:

those who can't afford to give, do give. Give best.
It hovers lightly, a frenzy to me
because I must imagine hovering,
my body heavier now after my child.

My son is the scent of water from a silver cup.
I pour my face out willingly
that he might see there constancy,
for lingering near is the bounded
water of a puddle, trees face down in it,
trees spoking in, the marked sky and strop
of bird trail across, clouds winching along.

And though I don't know, I believe
the heart has a scent too,
which is the scorch love generates.
That the heart with its pistons
goes *climb up and step*
down, climb-step, climb-step, and
in this way the holy minutes go by,
whether you love your day or not.

Tony Quagliano

Meanwhile I Just Said to Myself

"Meanwhile," I just said to myself,
"as I'm trying to write something about
how the Dominican sisters slapped
me around and everyone else I
went to grammar school with, and how
it used to mean nothing, but how
lately novels I've read
and movies I've seen
Eddie Coyle by Higgins, Breslin
Pacino in Scarecrow, even Dedalus in Portrait
slapped and knuckle-busted, victimized
by nuns and Jesuits
lately, have made newly
urgent, meaningful and
symbolic all that Dominican
slapdash discipline I merely took for granted
meanwhile
the cool semi-tropical dawn
has just broken over Diamond Head
a block and a half from my apartment
and a clatter of birds I could never name
just burst from a dozen trees
I know only as the coconut palms and
the assorted shorter ones

(Diamond Head is corny
unless you find yourself living there
five thousand miles from Brooklyn
an ecological ignoramus)
and the rain has started
swept leeward by the daily trades
which certainly will later sweep some
blue and white amazing sky
across this rock
and while the window runs
with rain and I watch the blurring
of the brooding cone beyond it
and in the next room, Laura
is still sleeping
I remind myself
that history, volcanic or my own
leads up to now, today
and though that article on nuns and novels
may have something in it
I think
right now
I'll write this poem instead."

Henry Rago

The Distances

This house, pitched now
The dark wide stretch
Of plains and ocean
To these hills over
The night-filled river,
Billows with night,
Swells with the rooms
Of sleeping children, pulls
Slowly from this bed,
Slowly returns, pulls and holds,
Is held where we
Lock all distances!

Ah, how the distances
Spiral from that
Secrecy:
Room,
Rooms, roof
Spun to the huge
Midnight, and into
The rings and rings of stars.

Vittoria Repetto

La Bella Figura

la bella figura
    dad believed in it
after mama died
    he tried to dress me
no s. klein, gimbels or macy's
for him
it was
lord & taylor's
bonwit teller
for me
    growing up mid 1960s
    off bleecker st.
it was the army-navy store
all I wanted was a pair of levi's
had to buy it myself
out of ten dollars allowance
as soon as the blue jeans got comfortable
you know
soft and faded
i'd come home open my closet
they'd be gone
happened every three months
his daughter shouldn't look like
a figlia di nessuno

nobody's child
i had to save up
not buy school lunch
nothing in the fridge
i ate pasta heros for weeks
now when I go for Sunday dinner
i wear blue jeans
if they're ripped
even better.

Lois Roma-Deeley

The Apostle of Wax and Shine

Parked in our driveway, the big finned
Lincoln sits like a fish
settling at the bottom of a basket
of so many passed-around loaves. As if its wide eyes,
open in death and crusted with chrome, went blind.

If St. Paul should ever lose his way
on this road that leads through 1959,
to my seven-year-old self sitting on the front steps
staring into the nothingness that would become my future,
he would find a rag top convertible, and my father
the Apostle of Wax and Shine.

Maybe he would come to understand a man
who's two months behind his $64-a-month house payment;
the black haired, squarish man, with strong teeth and sun-
tanned arms
who supports his wife, kids, no-good brother;
who makes the rounds, delivering bananas
in a small truck to little grocery stores
owned by immigrant Jews and Italians;
the sporting man whose name — *Lou* — is inscribed in script
on blue denim,
maybe Paul would cut the guy a break.

He might see a man whistling as he rubs the soft cloth
into paste wax and onto the white paint,
making circle inside of circles each and every time.
But does he see my own face in the reflection
gleaming off the hood of this car? See the wisdom

of four white walls which will spin
into spring, clearing a space across the days,
a very small place where I still live
simply for a little bit of magic?

Joe Ross

from An American Voyage

A gap.
Seven years wide and more.
At a loss of in between and less.
The stars studded in mixed inverted light.
Objects of worship washed in upon deserted shores.
When all is too suddenly—

Calm, brown —
flailing in green.

A long voyage against rock.
The beginning of angle.
Resonating within prism.

If you could bring the world
in a wide stare into white.
The arms opened wider than shoulders allow.
When sex is not sex.
This goes out.
Returned in so many others.

Up-turned in misplaced image.

Rubbing against the edge of it.

The stakes raised.
The roots pulled in brown sound.
A mixing together in dense community.
This land named in unknown call.
Breaking upon nearly deserted shores.

When this goes out.
When you begin.

Alone, washed in deserted recall.
You begin to think back.
A way through.
From the first voyage –
to this landing. A rock.
Tossed from sea to pool.
Our roots disturbed
from the clear reflection
scattered by the waves made
of so small pebble.

When home becomes only place.

Clare Rossini

The Diagrammer of Sentences

for my father

Beneath the kitchen's halo of fluorescence
I stood shyly at your side,
The pen in your big freckled fist
Filleting sentence after sentence,

Whether compound or not,
With all manner of tenses shivering,
And the phrase singled out, and the absolute exposed.

Music from the stove a few feet away,
My mother humming, pot lids clanking,

Above and below and around, cries and laughter —

Ten of us crammed into that bungalow
Braced against the winter riding in
From the frost-shorn fields.

Find the subject,
You said to me, *That's the proper start* —

Subject or object, which was I?

And then the predicate, with its verb —

To sing, to pray, to think, to be,
How could words contain such festering?

"To modify," you said, *Is to shape, to fix qualities to —*

Word-love infecting the air we breathed,
The dictionary presiding at supper
Night after night, a Prospero's book
Of roots and derivations,

And scraps of paper fluttering on the walls,
Poems, proscriptions, prayers,
Some in foreign tongues:

In medio stat virtue.

In bocca chiusa,
Non ci entra mosche.

Character is all.

Wind banged the house-side
As you looked sideways up, your eyes
Behind your thick black glasses
Studying my face.

Want to try? you asked, then turned back
To the blank white universe
Your hand held in place, printing a sentence there

With a flourish.

Did I take the pen,
Scatter your words on my own diagram's broken,
Sideways tree?

I remember the sentence
You made for me:

Gladly the man and his daughter walked up the hill.

Frank Samperi

from Anamnesis

moon   skyscrapers
moon   branches

blocked

blue everywhere
light ever
center
unseen
where yes
clearly
flower
not unlike
no

gardens
streets
not wretched
rather

state

projected

discoloring

sit in a park

otherworldly

therefore

to withdraw

from the literary world

is a must

this proves

our style no style

ars imitatur naturam

in sua operatione

it takes courage to go this way

because it is not the way of the world

I mean

the heretics

can no longer be

Luther

Bruno

Campanella

heresy is going against

the Material Ideal

and only the spiritual man can do that

but here going against

is innocuous

no trap

no argument

release

the Material Ideal not something to be destroyed

because the spiritual man not impeded

his movement reaps

enough daily to see thru

release even the Material Ideal

can there be a poetry of pace

no

people

no

no poetry that seeks to release

even the Material Ideal

can be dramatic

epical

or

lyrical

then what kind of poetry is left

given the Hegelian

the Marxist

there can be no poetry

because the upshot is

the Platonic user

maker

no imitator

therefore

the kind of poetry

we postulate

is the kind that resolves

book

canzone

song

what kind is that

theological poetry

on my way back

from my parttime job

I think

have I written malice
because I have failed
to give lip service
to the civil
there are the workers
breaking their backs
the traffic
complements them
I'm the same
only I refuse to submit
my revolt
is not to give in
to any desire
that ultimately leads
to a justification
position achieved
society more fully reformed

then there's the home
I return to my wife and children
their existences
tied up
in the scheme of things

surrounding
how do I alleviate the burdens
I don't
I can't
I'm just a worker
and what is even worse
a poet
who sees his poetry
as work
a means toward an end
do I desire
to be anything other
than a worker
no
thus the tragedy
of my movement
any worker's movement
but the dialectical
is not the thought process
I'm involved in
if involvement
therefore
process

can in no sense
take significance
from a logic
not referable
to application

what about the political situation
it's misleading
of course
it depends upon
your position
in society
how else can you represent
your particular view
no report
can ever claim
to be ubiquitous
therefore
the uselessness
of the reports
they simply reflect
the position's slant
and of course

the Material Ideal
is the better for it
because the solution of
all these slants lies
in the integral
that knows no differences

how far can we go
in our descent
toward particulars
not far
our language
mathematical
or otherwise
just reaps surfaces

Maria Sassi

Town Story

I heard this once — a story from the son
of one of the men who pulled her body out,
swollen and milky from grey creek water.
The stones in her apron, still intact,
sewn in with heavy button thread.

It was a day in late March when she walked in
. . . shoes and all . . . as if she were walking away
from something toward something else.

Mrs. D'Bella, the story goes, looked like
the beauty on the Medaglia D'Oro coffee can.
A young widow some Italian men in town
called "la donna misteriosa."

Her husband lost his life working on the
Newburgh bridge over the Hudson. Some said
he was a jealous man with an old country
temper — some said he adored her. They had
two children, a boy and a girl who were
in school at the time of their mother's
suicide. No one knows what happened to them.

The lived in one of the houses built on
a ledge above the creek that splits the town.
Long wooden steps went down to a narrowing
curve of mud flats — children fished there,
skated in winter. But in early spring
water rose to over twenty feet in the middle.

A note was never found. She must have stared
all morning down those steps, her eyes
moving slowly to the middle of the creek.
And she must have gone out there when out
of herself. Some other energy stitched
those shore stones in her apron — quickly —
lest the children come home early —
St. Mary's school only a block away.

Leslie Scalapino

from NEW TIME

wild gap — of dawn, not it — not so much the particular interpretation (of events) — but as (that) it happens at all

filled events (catalyzed in one as physical gap tormenting ? is itself the break that's the dawn, in fact) — break — expanded — that are going on — red flamed trees, leaves sea is the occurrence outside.

~ ~ ~

freezing sky — red slice — one, outside, travelling not existing even — is *not* not rebelling — gap itself — as choosing the harshest conditions — is the dawn

that is dusk freezing sky — is gap

grinding negative, as going down that's dusk sky — *per se* — one's pushing wildly occurring (in one) events — as gap, (that's dawn)

~ ~ ~

"seeing Venus in the morning sky" — (he's speaking)

(aggressive waves coming from someone one day — then from another person — to hit on oneself — who's, then, rebelling) — "I saw a white azalea — yesterday (morning too) — blooming in the whole space" (on rim?) — "I imagined yesterday — the next — the next — the next — is blooming" —

rim floating, wave that's someone's — *not* — (isn't) rebelling

~ ~ ~

white azalea blooming — 'I saw' — is — (someone's hitting, one day) again, it

rebelling as — not — (and) making — that thought form — that is the sky's dawn

coming in (impinging) on the line, (that's dawn) — figures, when kept out — admitted 'in to' it, diaphanous are the line/frame in one

are — *not* — rebelling — or not being outside even — as: freezing sky — itself — (people for whom one cares — their own — suffering which is time — dawn) — moving — no weight, and is admitted in one.

~ ~ ~

Jennifer Scappettone

An Abeyance

Being benched coast-
distant (drift has its intents) slow I to
sigh the careful flukes
of a sparse hundred a day these
encrusted nursers from
lagoons & their lousish peers
of elsewhere eyes
of a great, gray, two-thirds of the time, migration
against typewriter's of a sudden set
set the revelations at a desk on an anthill of Buzzardville
after which come flinging jawing genius's
sure barbell discs; brace yourself
barbell-in-the-head heard all day
in the lines of a supper, in the lines betwixt which
[and the typewriter]
a mute, taut portrait rotates,
utter in the round, languor's
the subject discovers, chews the articulations of mother —
chews on that a good white....
Leaping Lethe, thought's jawing
wave haha you can't
impercussively herd her outrageousness away
or surhunger author
fishwife of fishmonger

who're set to an earth
and its wanes, who
woo lush of sea
made scrupulous
in the world of do...

John Skoyles

FATHER COLOMBO

As a boy I went to church each week,
and listed sins to my favorite priest,
a goodnatured guy breastfed in Brooklyn,

whose smile wasn't cynical or coy
like the grins of archbishops,
and when he talked to God

his lips were surprisingly passionate.
Later I heard he left the church,
became a widow's exotic pet,

and summered on islands
with cool millionaires;
and I hoped it wasn't true,

because when I pictured him kissing
the powerful and rich,
he began to disappear,

like God did
when I tried to imagine
he always was, and always will be here.

Gilbert Sorrentino

The Memory

A smell of apricots that brings a place
to mind. To the eye. Words twist in the air
in tortured anagrams

shards fall into your life
that once had meaning

you think. You are arrested and your face
is brought to bear on all of it. This man

that man. A woman is in it somewhere
for the asking but the apricots overpower
you, the sentences clamor, voices,
voices.

The air shifts, you thought you were
in the street, you are in a room, what room
can it be, it seems familiar, it is full
of a distant smell, sweet and thin
and these anagrams

are falling into patterns, of course you
are in a room, this is a smell of apricots.

They bring a place
to mind. These voices are meaningless,
are tortured problems twisting in air.

Felix Stefanile

The Americanization of the Immigrant

Your words, Genoveffa,
through the open window,
telling me once again
what to buy at the store:
don't forget, don't forget —
aroma of fresh bread,
almost a halo.

That was a long time ago.
I never forgot.
Like Dante
I have pondered and pondered
the speech I was born with,
lost now, mother gone,
the whole neighborhood bulldozed,
and no one to say it on the TV,
that words are dreams.

John Tagliabue

GOOD FRIDAY IN PROCIDA

A boat
with my family
sailed before the dawn came
and it was still very dark and cold
to a small island near Ischia,
an island where there was a large Penitentiary
on a hill, and the beautiful sea and sky everywhere,
where this day, Good Friday, many people in black
remembered and re-enacted as still partly in the Dream
The Passion of the Lord, the Fisherman, the Sun.
They and we and maybe He walked past small stores
selling Easter bread and large lemons, past small dark eyes and caves,
walked slowly up as the dawn began to join us in our walking
the mysterious hill of the small colorful quiet radiant town
surrounded by the infinite and delicate beauty of the sea
now growing lighter even as the Child was radiant at his birth
and our always death. We went up partly as in a dream
the narrow winding ways by crowds of people part of the Passion
in black, the little houses in a dim and radiant pink or blue
or violet or yellow or white. We waited until the sound of death
as a cry from the bottom of roots or from a dead child or from a wound
of Christ entered the flower of the dawn and three eternal musicians
with instruments more primitive than man sounded the deep
sound of sorrow. It tore our hand. And then the procession began

and when and where it began and ended we do not know because
it is a play and a community of watchers and waiters and sufferers
and parents and children and bakers and butchers and priests and
prisoners
forever part of the waking heart since Adam carried the invisible tree
out of Eden and the cold sky wept like the flesh of Eve. The
beauty of man and woman there in the gray and shocking dawn of
our murder, though we are the murdered one too; the keeper of the
prisoner is not known
from the prisoner even as the sky is not known from our hand
now invisibly bleeding as the priests and the partakers and children
in the white of His Death walk unceremoniously down the winding way
to enter the Tomb of the Church. Voices like fish
or flowers or stones
were part of the sound of the day as in distance from above unseen
the Body of the Lord was approaching us. Women wept. And the bodies
of lambs
tied to a cross, the bodies of doves made into a cross, the children in
white
carrying crosses on their backs, many children in white carrying the
banquets of the Last Supper
with fish with flowers for eyes, and petals over their sparkling sea
rainbows went past us.
Mothers remembered the dying of their husbands and sons and for
hours the signs of the cross,
the signs of agony like the parts of Mankind
were separated and carried before us as food is broken as the Sun goes
dry hanging on the Tree.

And then the Body of Christ like a quiet and ever present burst of
flames
or birds in loss of migration in the body of our bleeding and lostness
summoned themselves to our vision and the eyes and doors and hands
of the Church:
and the heavy music played beyond all its funeral march coming to us
like Tragedy
and we saw made of the Tree made of Man Christ with his wounds
as we died on the street and the mothers and children and shadows
of the dead like the leaves entering the ground followed the
triumphant body
into the resurrection of the invisible Church, the invisible sea, the
invisible Sky, the ever visible wonder of You.

Aldo Tambellini

November 9, 1990

there is an ad on TV
selling a spray:
kill dandelions
the unwanted ugly weed

I take from the field
the stem holding
the dandelion seeds
blow into them
to disperse the seeds
over the land
for procreation

I pick the fresh
tender leaves
cut as the teeth of a lion

I taste the bitter roots
then thank mother earth
for this food
that sustained so many of us
from hunger

It's war time
the spring of '44
a homage
to a very dear plant
that is long overdue

Thom Tammaro

Richard M. Nixon: My Italian Problem*

Mr. Chairman, all of the distinguished guests on the platform,
and all of you gathered here in Stamford:

As I speak to you today with regard to this center,
I naturally have some comments with regard to this
Italian Center for Stamford, Connecticut.
I wish to speak on Columbus Day of what America
owes to those of Italian background,
the many that have contributed to this country

"The Italians. We mustn't forget the Italians.

On that point, I think that one indication of what we owe
we see right up here on this platform. ...
I want Secretary Volpe to stand up again.
John Volpe was Governor of your neighboring State of
    Massachusetts.
He has served as Secretary of Transportation for this
    administration.
He has handled many other assignments for us.
But one thing that always impressed me about John Volpe
is the way that he speaks so movingly of his background.
He is proud that he is a first-generation Italian-American.
He is proud of that background and justly so.

We mustn't forget the Italians. Must do something for them.
They're not, we ah … they're not like us.

When I was in Rome just a week, 2 weeks ago,
I recall that as we spoke in that great city,
that one of my Italian friends there said there were
twice as many Italians living in America as live in Rome,
8 ½ million. I was thinking not only of the number
of those of Italian background who live in America,
8 ½ million, but of the long history that we have
of those of Italian background and what they
have contributed to America.
Everyone knows this is Columbus Day.
We also know that through the years
those of Italian background in all areas
in the field of science,
in music,
in art,
in business,
in government,
have made their contributions
to America's greatness.

Be proud of the fact that your parents or your grandparents were Italian,

After all, you can't blame them. Oh no … can't do that.
They've never had the things we've had.

Finally, Mr. Chairman, I would like to speak
in a very personal vein about the heritage

that we owe to those of Italian background,
not simply Christopher Columbus, the navigator
who found the New World,
and not Enrico Fermi, the man who found another new world
along with other scientists, the breaking of the secret
with regard to nuclear power.

Difference is, the ... They smell different, look different, act different.

But I think of what happened recently in the world of sports
that to all of us who follow sports moved us very greatly.

I think of Vince Lombardi and what he meant.
We think of him as a great coach ...
What he stood for basically was something
that every young person in this audience particularly,
I know, will want to stand for.
He stood for character.
He stood for strength.
He believed deeply in his family,
in his church,
and in whatever cause he was involved.
He believed that a man had to become involved
in a cause deeper, bigger than himself
in order to reach the fulfillment of all of his talents.

Difference is, the ...
They smell different,

look different,
act different.

After all, you can't blame them.

I simply say, as I dedicate this center,

We mustn't forget the Italians.
Must do something for them.
They're not, we ah …
They're not like us.
Difference is, the …
They smell different,
look different,
act different.
After all, you can't blame them.
Oh no … can't do that.
They've never had the things we've had.

Let us think back to the history of America.
Let us think of all of those who came across the seas,
at very great sacrifice, to this country
and then helped to make it greater.
And then let us think of what we have.
That is what Americans stand for.
That is what we are here for.

The Italians.
We mustn't forget the Italians …
After all, you can't blame them

I dedicate this center to that cause.

Of course, the trouble is . . .
the trouble is
you can't find one that's honest

Thank you.

*All words taken from the transcripts of Richard Nixon's remarks at the dedication of the Italian Community Center in Stamford, Connecticut, October 12, 1970, and from the Watergate Tapes, in a 1970 conversation between Nixon and his adviser John Ehrlichman.

Joanne Tangorra

Photograph, 1920

for Margherita D'Andrea, 1884-1964

Fisted mitts of dried cheese
strung up like offerings
in the window
of my grandfather's store.

Petition or sacrifice:
these are the choices

this summer day
when my grandmother
takes a break
from the dairy business
on a sidewalk in the Bronx.

She sits
for a minute
on a chair she has pulled into the sun
a child on her lap,

her white apron creased
like a new map unfolded, open

to the din of voices
thick with vowels, anise-scented
streets and bells of Mt. Carmel
chiming each hour.

Faith intrigues the faithless who cannot
take that *beautiful risk* and believe

the soul immortal —

my grandmother's photograph
on a wall where she would have hung instead the dark
wooden crucifix she carried
country to country parting

seas of doubt to alight on a future
before it washed over her

a wave
that wiped clean the sand
its brief scrawl of names

her oldest daughter's
willful death by drowning

and knowing
not even the mother tongue
could save her.

Still years from that moment
my grandmother looks into the camera far
from her own mother deep
in the heel
of their boot-shaped country.

Her shoes are laced
tight to the ankles
and she wears black
stockings even in summer

even in this new world her feet
placed squarely on pavement.

Maria Terrone

GHOST FRESCOES

Basilica of San Zeno Maggiore, Verona

A chubby fist and wing
float free, severed
from the landscape of human affairs.

Below, a barefoot saint
seems to straddle acres, beaming
casual self-possession, the divine

right to stake eternal claim – but
in the space between
both legs, a third intrudes,

last remnant of a man fading
to white dust. Nine hundred years ago
this wall was his. Reduced

to a toehold, he now spites
the fourteenth-century arriviste,
holding his ground with the ghost

of what he was. The saint remains
oblivious. Centuries sweep
around him like planets' rings;

the church's wheel-of-fortune
spins rose light
through plague and war.

Yet so vivid
are his blue and russet robes,
he glistens — a refugee

from a sun shower
who's arrived dripping wet, an idea
fresh from the brush of his maker.

Joseph Torra

Self-Portrait With A Loaf of Bread

Who says you knead mud to bake bread? That ice pick I snipped from a past life was once used in an attempted murder. A stranger approached me on the street, an aged fellow who had trouble speaking. *Gather up your surplus into your heart* he blurted out several times.

There is an inward division of selves, among place. Laced tortoise-shelled markings. Each morning the corral of a good night's rest. We own more verbs than space which some say attributes unequal growth and a desensitizing effect which activates when the climate is right and too much yeast is added. What this illustrates I know. Wrench expression. Break mask. Ferret underground past.

Catherine Tufariello

Keeping My Name

"T as in Tom . . .U . . . F as in Frank,"
I tell the voice at the bookstore or the bank,
Knowing the chances of its being right
On form or package are extremely slight
Unless the clerk repeats (and most don't bother)
This catechism I learned from my father —
T as in Tom, U, F as in Frank.
For this ritual I have myself to thank —
Twice I've had and forfeited the chance
To trade the burden and extravagance
Of five syllables for one or two.
I couldn't do it when I said "I do,"
Not even after three years in the South,
Where voweled names are mangled in the mouth.
What's in a name? Why, a family line,
Identity, tradition, but in mine
I had the gallop of the Latin dactyl;
Tufa, crumbly stuff, so richly tactile,
So unlike Grandpa's monumental granite;
And, from the intrepid who could scan it,
I had the liquid lilting of *iello*
(One teacher sang it sweetly as a cello);
And those plump vowels, juicy and alive —
At one per syllable, I had all five.
In school, through endless dreamy afternoons,

I brooded like a druid casting runes
Over the page to see how many words
My name would make, releasing them like birds
From the magician's cloak I always wore.
Every year they multiplied, to more
Than I'd thought possible, as *rat* and *tale,*
Tall and *tell* gave way to *trill* and *flail,*
If and *far* to *float, aloft* and *lift.*
One day a *rill* might bubble from a *rift,*
The next an *elf* warble a silver *lute,*
A leering *troll* swig *ale* or proffer *fruit,*
One taste of which might lead to *fault* and *fall.*
They scattered, and I catalogued them all:
Found *fore* and *after,* leaping *fire* and *air*
(With sandstone, all the elements were there),
Caught *Uriel,* Milton's angel of the sun,
Wearing cloudy *tulle,* and the (nearly done),
Bright *Ariel,* Will Shakespeare's airy sprite,
Hidden in the middle, in plain sight —
Caught him in my net, then let him go,
Happy in his charms as Prospero.

Lewis Turco

An Immigrant Ballad

My father came from Sicily
(O sing a roundelay with me)
With cheeses in his pocket and
A crust of black bread in his hand.
He jumped ashore without a coat,
Without a friend or enemy,
Till Jesus nailed him by the throat.

My father came to Boston town
(O tongue a catch and toss one down).
By day he plied a cobbler's awl,
By night he loitered on the mall.
He swigged his wine, he struck his note,
He wound the town up good and brown,
Till Jesus caught him by the throat.

He'd heard of Hell, he knew of sin
(O pluck that wicked mandolin),
But they were for the gentle folk,
The cattle broken to the yoke.
He didn't need a Cross to tote:
His eyes were flame, his ears were tin,
Till Jesus nabbed him by the throat.

He met a Yankee girl one day
(O cry a merry roundelay)
Who wouldn't do as she was bid,
But only what the good folk did.
She showed him how the church bells peal
Upon the narrow straitaway,
And Jesus nipped him by the heel.

My father heard a sermon said
(O bite the bottle till it's dead).
He quit his job and went to school
And memorized the Golden Rule.
He drained his crock and sold his keg,
He swept the cobwebs from his head,
And Jesus hugged him by the leg.

The girl was pleased: She'd saved a soul
(O light a stogie with a coal).
No longer need she be so wary:
Daddy went to seminary
To find how warm a Yankee grows
When she achieves her fondest goal.
And Jesus bit him on the nose.

At last he had a frock to wear
(O hum a hymn and lip a prayer).
He hoisted Bible, sailed to search
For sheep to shear and for a church.
He asked the girl to share his life,

His choir-stall and shirt of hair,
For Jesus bade him take a wife.

My father holds a pulpit still
(O I have had enough to swill).
His eye is tame, his hair is gray,
He can't recall a roundelay.
But he can preach, and he can quote
A verse or scripture, as you will,
Since Jesus took him by the throat.

Joseph Tusiani

Song Of The Bicentennial

I.

What would my life have been
had I remained where I was born? What dreams
would I be dreaming now? I cannot even
compare my human state
with that of a plant plucked
from its salubrious ground
and placed elsewhere under a roof for heaven.
Just as the high decree of Fate to me,
incomprehensible
my every question will forever be
to the eternal unity of all —
mountain and rock that form it,
ocean and waves that make it, clouds and sky,
and sun and light. Sunder all this — you have
erosion, desert, and abyss and night.
Yet I have ceased to be
the man I was; the roots wherefrom I sprung
are somewhere else instead. Deracinated —
is this the word that somewhat hides the grief
of one uprooted and no longer young?

What would my life be now
if I were still with my familiar trees?

II.

Let me tonight be wondering about
the shape of every star —
not the unbounded magma that confounds
my human thinking that at best is doubt

nor the translucent sounds
that from the center of infinities
charge the celestial bodies near and far,
creating suns beyond the sun I know.

The shape — let me be wondering about
the shape of stars that glow,
for something tells me that I too was born
under the sign of one
formed like an ocean liner going far,
crowded with silent men called emigrants —
my ethnic star.

III.

Do I regret my origin by speaking
this language I acquired? Do I renounce,
by talking now in terms of only dreams,
the sogni of my childhood? What has changed
that I had thought unchangeable in me?
Yet something's changed — and what, I do not know.
Now every thought I think, each word I say

detaches me a little more from all
I used to love — your faces, ancient friends,
and all our phrases of so much delight
as needed no translation in my mind.

Mother, I even wonder if I am
the child I was, the little child you knew,
for you did not expect your little son
to grow apart from all that was your world,
the world that he saw first with your own eyes —
simple and untranslatable, composed
of one unclouded clarity of light.
Yet of a sudden he was taught to say
'Mother' for Mamma, and for cielo 'sky'.
That very day, we lost each other. Now
I know you look at me as though I were
a little more and yet a little less
than what a son — your little child — should be.
Oh, they have taught me to translate all things —
even my very self — into some new
and old infinity of roots and boughs,
so that I wonder whether I am old
or whether I am new beneath the sky,
beneath the cielo of my long-lost land.

IV.

My long-lost land was one that,
when snows enveloped it,
did not erase a sun that
still in my dream was lit.

But simple was the dream that
in all my fancy shone —
as simple as a gleam that
speaks of a sunken sun:

papier-mâché instead of
true shepherds, painted moss
for a pre-April meadow,
for living light the gloss

of crayon exercises
in every corner glued:
there, made of many sizes,
my cosmic marvel stood.

'Twas my presepe, full of
tu scendi dalle stelle —
the only song and rule of
intime cose belle.

But now my new-found land is
the western world, this new,
mysterious Atlantis
where men like me and you,

called immigrants, are silent
when Silent Night is sung
on this Manhattan Island
by people old and young,

by all save those, like me
and you, uprooted friend,
who think of Italy —
our lost presepe land.

V.

Two languages, two lands, perhaps two souls?
I dare not ask these flowers I know well,
each of them making its one calyx bright.
Nor can I question that forbidding oak:
though low and long, its roots
cease at the hindrance of the nearest brook
as if abhorring alienness of ground.
Then, who will solve the riddle of my day?
Two languages, two lands, perhaps two souls...
Am I a man or two strange halves of one?
Somber, indifferent light,
setting before me with a sneer of glow,

because there is no answer to my plight
I find some solace only in this thought —
that maybe, just as this revolving earth
must not proclaim your triumph all at once,
I too must be, while waiting for my dawn,
the night of my own self.
Or maybe, just as your unbridled flame
would, undivided, scald this hemisphere
and turn it into ashes, I fulfill
my human fate by giving you, O sun,
a chance of mercy on my helpless life.

VI.

Civis Americanus Sum: I swore
allegiance to the Flag of Fifty Stars:
long live America for ever more!

Now I belong where countless wounds and scars
create a morning and an epic song
that neither time nor silence ever mars.

Now, only now for every suffered wrong
do I discover who I am at last —
the multitudinous Italian throng.

I am the present for I am the past
of those who for their future came to stay,
humble and innocent and yet outcast.

I am the dream of their eternal day —
the dream they dreamed in mines bereft of light —
I am their darkness and their only ray,

their silence and their voice: I speak and write
because they dreamed that I would write and speak
about their unrecorded death and night.

O glory! I'm the bread they came to seek,
the vine they planted to outvanquish doom,
their most majestic and enduring peak.

For this my life their death made ample room.

Paul Vangelisti

After Ennio Correnti, 1948-1997

Even if the piazzas are currently empty
noticeably unopened like books on a shelf,
notwithstanding the carelessness of friendship
insisted on weeks sometimes years at a time,
or maybe just the ragged edge of summer
currently overcharging the skin with rash
or the progress of remorse and dripping faucets
running an indifferent blue through the quiet
reckless afternoon with nobody at home
every window shuttered, yesterday's mailman
noticeably younger, the mail undelivered
till six tomorrow morning, the lock on the door
impossible without playing with the key.

Pasquale Verdicchio

THE WAY HOME

In the corridor of dialogue
a turn may be mine

to retrace a doubt
against the back of the chair

hard spine and a jump
where the astray might be

from one continent back
and this is what home was

because it has been pushed back
and it becomes where home is

with a different name
but a familiar call

the misstep a shift
and take up residence

in a past city a past life
a momentary distraction or not

you take advantage of it
and find comfort in it

the shortest way home.

Paul Violi

From The Hazards of Imagery

At The Cottage of Messer Violi

The mailbox, painted dark blue,
sits atop a tilted cedar post.
It has a little red flag on one side
and it is altogether remarkable.

The Toyota in the driveway
is very old and is said
to have come from Japan.

There is in the hallway
an immense dogfood bowl.
It is made of iridescent pink plastic.
It is, as I have said, immense
and it is hideous.

In the kitchenette is a statuette
of Ceres, Goddess of Wheaties.

The dishwasher is a Kenmore
and altogether worthy of praise.

In the foyer the oversized painting
of a pork chop provides
visitors many opportunities
for conversation.

In the servants' quarters
there are many impressive works
that stress the imminence of death
and the probability of hellfire.

Placed on the broad maplewood table
beside bottles of cognac
there is a recording device
with a silver megaphone
into which natives are often
invited to shout
the oral histories of their people.

We whose hearts have been gripped
by life, scoff at the idea of art
as mere ornamentation: So they
seem to proclaim,
the three statues that adorn
the neighbor's lawn, plaster deer
with real bulletholes in them.

Robert Viscusi

PICTURE OF A MAN WITH A BROKEN HEART

In English we say Padua; in Italian, Padova.
In Italian, Basilica di Sant'Antonio; in English, Church of
 Saint Anthony.
Around the tomb of Saint Anthony in Padua stands an altar.
Around that altar people have left pictures of their parts.
"Saint Anthony healed my arm, and here is a silver arm."
Hammered silver arms hang at all angles, thousands of them.
The cloister museum has hundreds of feet, eyeballs, knees.
Sant'Antonio di Padova, finder of lost things, also heals the sick.
Padova is the seat of an ancient school of medicine.
Many paintings record accidents miraculously survived.
Ex voto. Because of a vow. Each piece records a vow.
"In gratitude for healing my heart, I send this picture."
Some paintings are of children restored to happiness.
There is a plaster cast of two hands.
People send their wedding rings.
Nothing is too small for Saint Anthony.
He will help you find your glasses, if they are what you need.
The picture is at the end of a corridor.
The man is painted looking straight ahead at the viewer.
Above him the heart, whole and aglow.
These rooms have skylights.

A row of silver hearts frames the painting.
In late afternoon silver is golden.
With his left hand, the man is pointing to the old heart.
It lies broken into huge humps of stone.
Artists call this gesture The Confession.
With his right hand the man points to the new heart.
Its red gold aureole distills the afternoon light.
Artists call this gesture The Vow.
Many of the paintings have Saint Anthony in them.
Others seem to be looking at him as if he were standing inside
you.
"Thank you for healing me," they say. "Thank you for finding
my glasses."

Notes on Contributors

KIM ADDONIZIO'S fifth poetry collection is *Lucifer at the Starlite* (2009). Her collection *Tell Me* (2000) was a National Book Award Finalist. Her first novel, *Little Beauties*, was published in 2005, and she has also authored two instructional books on writing poetry: *The Poet's Companion* (1997, with Dorianne Laux), and *Ordinary Genius: A Guide for the Poet Within* (2009).

JOE AMATO is the author of *Once an Engineer: A Song of the Salt City* (2009) and *Industrial Poetics: Demo Tracks for a Mobile Culture* (2006) and other books. He teaches at Illinois State University in Normal.

MICHAEL ANANIA'S recent books include *In Natural Light* (1999) and *Heat Lines* (2006). His work has recently received the Charles T. Angoff Award and the Aniello Lauri Award.

CHRISTOPHER ARIGO is the author of two books of poetry: *Lit interim* (2003) and *In the archives* (2007). He teaches at Washington State University and is co-editor of the literary journal *Interim* with poet Claudia Keelan.

ANNY BALLARDINI lives in Bolzano, Italy. She teaches high school; edits an online poetry site; and writes a blog: *Narcissus Works*. She is the author of two collections of poems, most recently *Dance in 33 Movements* (2009).

J. T. BARBARESE teaches at Rutgers University, Camden. He is the author of five volumes of poetry including *Very Small World* (2004) and *The Black Beach* (2005).

DENNIS BARONE is the author of a study of Italian American narrative entitled *America / Trattabili* (2011), *Parallel Lines*, a volume of selected poems (2011), and *Field Report*, a book of stories (2011). He is Director of American Studies at Saint Joseph College in West Hartford, CT.

DOROTHY BARRESI is the author of four books of poetry: *American Fanatics*; *Rouge Pulp*; *The Post-Rapture Diner*, winner of an American Book Award; and *All of the Above*, winner of the Barnard College New Women Poets Award. She is a Professor of English and Creative Writing at California State University, Northridge.

JOSEPH BATHANTI is Professor of Creative Writing at Appalachian State University in Boone, NC, and he is the author of six books of poetry, including *Restoring Sacred Art* (2010) as well as works of fiction and non-fiction.

JAMES BERTOLINO'S tenth volume of poetry is *Finding Water, Holding Stone* (2009). He is retired and lives outside Bellingham, Washington.

RAYMOND L. BIANCHI is a native of Chicago and he is the publisher of Cracked Slab Books. He has published three collections of poetry, most recently *Immediate Empire* (2008).

JOHN BRANDI has been faithful to the craft of poetry, painting, and journaling for the majority of his life. A recipient of numerous awards, he is an ardent traveler, with over thirty books published in the U.S. and abroad, among them *Facing High Water* (2008).

STEPHEN CAMPIGLIO is the program associate for Credit-Free Programs at Manchester Community College in Connecticut, where he also founded and coordinates the Mishi-maya-gat Spoken Word & Music Series. He was the featured poet in the summer 2008 issue of *Italian Americana*.

KARA CANDITO has an MFA from the University of Maryland and is currently a PhD student in creative writing at Florida State University. She is the author of *Taste of Cherry*, winner of the 2008 Prairie Schooner Book Prize.

MARY CAPONEGRO is the Richard B. Fisher Family Professor in Literature and Writing at Bard College. She has been a visiting artist at the American Academy in Rome and she has received the Rome Prize Fellowship in Literature. Her latest book of fiction is *All Fall Down*.

DAVID CAPPELLA is the author of *Gobbo: A Solitaire's Opera* (2004) and has co-authored with Baron Wormser two books on the writing of poetry: *A Surge of Language: Teaching Poetry Day by Day* (2004) and *Teaching the Art of Poetry: The Moves* (2000). He teaches at Central Connecticut State University.

EMANUEL CARNEVALI (1898-1942), published only one book during his lifetime, *A Hurried Many* (1925), yet he remains a familiar, though tragic, figure in literary Modernism. The poem included here he once told Ezra Pound he thought his best. Richard Johns published this poem in *Pagany* (Fall 1930).

CHRISTINE CASSON is Scholar/Writer in Residence at Emerson College, and she is the author of *After the First World* (2008).

GRACE CAVALIERI'S *Water on the Sun* won the 2005 Bordighera Poetry Award. Her volume *Anna Nicole: Poems* received a 2009 Paterson Award for Literary Excellence. Cavalieri founded "The Poet and the Poem" on public radio, now celebrating its thirty-third year on air.

JOSEPH CERAVOLO (1934-1988), the first recipient of the Frank O'Hara Award for Poetry, published several collections of poetry before his early death. In 1994 Coffee House Press published a selected poems and Wesleyan University Press will publish a complete poems.

JOHN CIARDI (1916-1986) authored more than forty volumes of poetry, including *The Collected Poems of John Ciardi* (1997). Ciardi is perhaps best known for *How Does a Poem Mean?* (1959), which became a text in high school and college classes. He also remains well-remembered for his impressive version of Dante's *Divine Comedy*.

DAVID CITINO (1947-2005) authored thirteen books, including *The News and Other Poems* (2002) and *A History of Hands* (2006). He taught for many years at Ohio State University where he directed the creative writing program from 1986-1993 and was the university poet laureate.

NED CONDINI, writer, translator, and literary critic, received the PEN/Poggioli Award for his versions of poet Mario Luzi and the Bordighera Prize for his rendering of Jane Tassi's *ANDSONGSONGSONGLESSNESS.* He recently published a novel, *The Cauldron* (2008), and the MLA *Anthology of Modern and Contemporary Italian Poetry* (2009).

GREGORY CORSO (1930-2001), a central figure in the Beat Generation literary movement, published seven books of poetry including *Mindfield: New & Selected Poems* (1989). At the time of Corso's death, Robert Creeley said, "Lots of us propose to be poets but who finally stakes all, or just takes all, as being that way? In my lifetime only Robert Duncan could be his equal in this way. It was honor indeed to have had his company."

PAOLA CORSO has published one book of poetry *Death by Renaissance* (2004) and one book of fiction *Giovanna's 86 Circles and Other Stories* (2007). She teaches at Western Connecticut State University.

GERALD COSTANZO is Professor of English at Carnegie Mellon University where he founded the University's press in 1975. For twenty years he edited *Three Rivers Poetry Journal.*

PETER COVINO'S *Cut Off the Ears of Winter* received the 2007 PEN/Osterweil Award. He is a founding editor of *Barrow Street*, poetry editor of *Voices in Italian Americana*, and teaches in the English Department at the University of Rhode Island.

PELLEGRINO D'ACIERNO (1882-1950), Italian born physician-poet, died while treating a patient. At the time of his death he was chief obstetrician and gynecologist of North Hudson Hospital in New Jersey.

PASCAL D'ANGELO (1894-1932) published an extraordinary immigrant autobiography in 1924, *Son of Italy.* He interspersed poems throughout it. Although he had some success as a poet in the mid-twenties, he died destitute, penniless. "The Toilers" appeared in *The Literary Digest* in October 1922 on the same page as poems by Edna St. Vincent Millet and Rudyard Kipling.

RACHEL GUIDO DEVRIES is the author of *The Altar Boy of Limbo* (2007), *Gambler's Daughter* (2001), and other books. She lives in Cazenovia, New York where she teaches and is a poet-in-the-schools.

RAY DIPALMA'S recent books include *The Ancient Use of Stone* and *Pensieri* (both 2009). He teaches Literature and Writing at the School of Visual Arts in New York City.

DIANE DI PRIMA is the author of forty-three books of poetry and prose, including *Pieces of a Song* (1990) and an expanded edition of *Revolutionary Letters* (2007). She has received an Award for Lifetime Achievement in Poetry from the National Poetry Foundation. In 2009 she became poet laureate of San Francisco.

JOHN DOMINI'S novel *A Tomb on the Periphery* (2008) made the short list at the London Book Festival for "the best of international publishing," and his novel *Earthquake I.D.*, in Italian translation, was the runner-up for the 2009 Domenico Rea prize.

ELAINE EQUI'S books include *The Cloud Of Knowable Things* (2003), *Ripple Effect: New and Selected Poems* (2007), and *Click and Clone* (2011). She teaches in the MFA programs at The New School and The City College of New York.

LAWRENCE FERLINGHETTI, a prominent voice of the poetry movement that began in the 1950s, has written poetry, translation, fiction, theater, art criticism, film narration, and essays. Often concerned with social issues, Ferlinghetti's poetry counters the literary elite's definition of art and the artist's role in the world. Among his recent books is *Poetry As Insurgent Art* (2007).

VINCENT FERRINI (1913-2007) published his first book of poems, *No Smoke*, in 1941. He published more than twenty additional volumes of verse, edited the magazine *Four Winds*, and was poet laureate of Gloucester, Massachusetts.

DIANA FESTA is the author of four books of literary criticism and five volumes of poetry, including *The Gathering* (2009). She is the recipient of a Guggenheim fellowship and the Guizot Award from the French Academy.

JONATHAN GALASSI is President and Publisher of Farrar, Straus and Giroux. He is the author of *North Street and Other Poems* (2000) and he has published several volumes of translations of the Italian poet Eugenio Montale, including *Collected Poems: 1920-1954* (1998).

MARY GIAIMO held an artist residency in Martignano, Italy during the month of August, 2010. Previously, she has lived in Florence for four years where she was a creative writing teacher and a travel writer for *Vista* magazine.

DAVID GIANNINI'S most recent book is *AZ II* (2006). *Sum Of Thread*, his book of prose poems is forthcoming.

SANDRA M. GILBERT, Distinguished Professor of English Emerita at the University of California, Davis, is the author of seven collections of poetry. *Belongings* (2005) is her latest book of poetry. A former president of the Modern Language Association, Gilbert co-authored with Susan Gubar *The Madwoman in the Atic: The Woman Writer and the 19th-Century Literary Imagination*, and *No Man's Land: The Place of the Woman Writer in the 20th Century.*

MARIA MAZZIOTTI GILLAN won the American Book Award for her book, *All That Lies Between Us* (2008). Her most recent book is *What We Pass On: Collected Poems* (2010). She is Executive Director of the Poetry Center at Passaic County Community College in Paterson, NJ, Director of the Creative Writing Program and Professor of Poetry at Binghamton University, SUNY, and editor of the *Paterson Literary Review.*

DANA GIOIA, former Chairman of the National Endowment of the Arts, has published three collections of poetry. His collection, *Interrogations at Noon*, received the 2002 American Book Award. An influential critic as well, Gioia's

1991 volume *Can Poetry Matter?* was a finalist for the National Book Critics Circle award.

JOHN GIORNO is an artist and musician as well as a poet. Giorno's fifty-year career, intertwined with contemporaries such as Andy Warhol and William S. Burroughs, has been characterized by high-energy performances and social activism.

DANIELA GIOSEFFI is a pioneering Italian American woman writer, critic, and editor. Her anthology *Woman on War* received the American Book Award in 1990. She has been given a Lifetime Achievement Award from the Association of Italian American Educators and the John Ciardi Lifetime Achievement Award in Poetry. Her latest book of poems is a bilingual edition titled *Blood Autumn, Autunno di sangue* (2006).

ARTURO GIOVANNITTI (1884-1959) emigrated from Italy to the United States in 1904. He was a writer, editor, and labor organizer, and began writing in English in 1911. He participated in many strikes and many of the poems in his 1914 book *Arrows in the Gale*, including the 1912 poem "The Bum," were strike related and inspired.

PETER GIZZI'S books include *Some Values of Landscape and Weather* (2003). He currently serves as poetry editor for the *Nation* and teaches at the University of Massachusetts.

ROSE BASILE GREEN (1914-2003) – scholar, poet, professor – is perhaps best known for her important study: *The Italian American Novel: A Document of the Interaction of Two Cultures* (1974). She was a founder of Cabrini College in Radnor, Pennsylvania and taught there from 1957-1970.

GEORGE GUIDA has published two volumes of poetry: *New York and Other Lovers* (2008) and *Low Italian* (2006). He is also the author of *The Peasant and the Pen* (2003), a volume of critical essays on Italian-American literature.

GERRY LAFEMINA is the author of two books of prose poems, a book of short stories, and five collections of poems, including *The Parakeets of Brooklyn* (2005). He directs the Lyric Center for Creative Writing at Frostburg State University.

TERESA LEO is the author of *The Halo Rule* (2008), winner of the Elixir Press Editors' Prize. Her poems have appeared in *The American Poetry Review*, *Poetry*, and *Ploughshares*. She works at the University of Pennsylvania.

P. H. LIOTTA is Professor of Humanities and Executive Director of the Pell Center for International Relations and Public Policy, Salve Regina University. He is a former Fulbright Artist-in-Residence in Yugoslavia and he has received the Robert H. Winner Memorial Award from the Poetry Society of America.

GIAN LOMBARDO is editor and publisher of Quale Press and publisher in residence at Emerson College. He is author or translator of many works of poetry including his recent book *Who Lets Go First* (2010).

MATTHEW LONGABUCCO teaches in the Language and Thinking Program at Bard College and in the Liberal Studies Program at New York University. His poems have appeared in *Conduit*, *Pleiades*, *Washington Square*, and elsewhere.

ALESSANDRA LYNCH is the author of two books of poetry: *Sails the Wind Left Behind* (2002) and *It was a terrible cloud at twilight* (2008). She teaches poetry at Butler University.

ANNE MARIE MACARI'S most recent book is *She Heads Into the Wilderness* (2008). Her first book, *Ivory Cradle* (2000), won the APR/Honickman First Book Prize in Poetry. She is also the author of *Gloryland* (2005) and she is the director of the Drew University Low-Residency MFA Program in Poetry and Poetry in Translation.

GERARD MALANGA, poet, photographer, filmmaker, was a major part of Andy Warhol's studio, known as The Factory. Among his many books of poetry are *Mythologies of the Heart* (1996) and *No Respect: New and Selected Poems 1964-2000* (2001).

SARAH MANGUSO is the author most recently of the highly acclaimed memoir *The Two Kinds of Decay* (2008) as well as the short story collection *Hard to Admit and Harder to Escape* (2007), and two books of poetry: *Siste Viator* (2006) and *The Captain Lands in Paradise* (2002). Among her honors is the Joseph Brodsky Rome Fellowship at the American Academy in Rome.

MARY ANN MANNINO teaches at Temple University. She is the author of *Revisionary Identities: Strategies of Empowerment in the Writing of Italian American Women* (2000). Her poems have appeared in the *Alabama Review*, the *Paterson Literary Review*, and *Voices in Italian Americana.*

PAUL MARIANI received the 2009 John Ciardi Award for Lifetime Achievement in Poetry. He is a poet, biographer, critic, and currently holds a Chair in Poetry at Boston College.

DONNA MASINI teaches in the MFA Creative Writing Program at Hunter College. She is the author of the novel *About Yvonne* (1997) and the volume of poems *Turning to Fiction* (2004).

CAROLE MASO is an English Professor at Brown University. She is the author of numerous cross-genre, innovative works such as *Defiance* (1999) and *The Room Lit by Roses* (2002).

STEPHEN MASSIMILLA is a poet, literary critic, painter, and former co-manager of an art gallery. He received an MFA and a PhD from Columbia University, where he now teaches classics and modernist literature. He is the author of *Forty Floors from Yesterday* (2002).

JEROME MAZZARO is the author of five books of poetry including *Weathering the Changes* (2002) and *Dream Catchers* (2008). He has published numerous volumes of criticism as well and lives in New York City.

ALBERT MOBILIO is the recipient of a Whiting Writers' award. His books of poetry include *Me with Animal Towering* (2002). He is an assistant professor of literary studies at the New School's Eugene Lang College.

STEPHEN MURABITO is an associate professor of English at the University of Pittsburgh at Greensburg. He is the author of the book-length poem *The Oswego Fugues* (2005), the volume of poems *The Communion of Asiago* (2006), and author and editor of the composition reader *Connections, Contexts, and Possibilities* (2001).

MICHAEL PALMA has published many translations of modern and contemporary Italian poets. In 2002 his terza rima translation of Dante's *Inferno* was published. He has received the Raiziss/de Palchi Fellowship and the Raiziss/de Palchi Book Prize from the Academy of American Poets.

MICHAEL PALMER, poet and translator, has worked with Margaret Jenkins Dance Company for over thirty years and has collaborated with many visual artists and composers. His most recent poetry collections are *Codes Appearing: Poems 1979-1988* (2001) and *Company of Moths* (2005). In 2006, he received the Wallace Stevens Prize from the Academy of American Poets.

JOSEPH PAPALEO (1926-2004) founded the Creative Writing Program at Sarah Lawrence College where he taught until his retirement. He authored three works of fiction: *All the Comforts* (1967), *Out of Place* (1970), and *Italian Stories* (2002).

JAY PARINI is a poet, novelist, biographer, and critic. He teaches at Middlebury College and in 2009 he published a volume of essays called *Why Poetry Matters*.

LUCIA PERILLO has published five volumes of poems, most recently *Inseminating the Elephant* (2009), a finalist for the Pulitzer Prize. She is a former MacArthur fellow and her book of essays, *I've Heard the Vultures Singing*, is now out in paperback.

ANTHONY PICCIONE (1939-2001) taught for twenty-five years at the State University of New York at Brockport. He published his third book with BOA Editions, *For the Kingdom*, in 1997.

NICK PIOMBINO is the author of many works of poetry, most recently *Contradicta: Aphorisms* (2010) which includes one hundred collaged illustrations by Toni Simon.

FRANK POLITE (1936-2005) published his work in magazines and journals such as *Harper's*, *The Nation*, *The North American Review*, *Poetry*, and *Yankee*. His books include *Flamingo* (1990) and *HYDE* (2004). "Last Part of the Interview" is from *Letters of Transit* (1979).

LIA PURPURA is the author of three collections of poems, three collections of essays, and one collection of translations. *On Looking* (essays, 2006) was a finalist for the National Book Critics Circle Award. She is currently Writer in Residence at Loyola University in Baltimore and teaches in the low-residency Rainier Writing Workshops.

TONY QUAGLIANO (1941-2007) published widely in literary journals, and published four books of poetry, including *pictographs* (2008). *Language Matters* is forthcoming. He was editor of *KAIMANA*, the journal of the Hawai'i Literary Arts council, and he was a contributing editor to the *Pushcart Prize: Best of the Small Presses* for thirty-three years. "Meanwhile I Just Said To Myself" originally appeared in the *Mid-Atlantic Review* (1975).

HENRY RAGO (1915-1969) was a poet and editor of *Poetry Magazine* for fourteen years from 1955-1969. He was also a Professor of Theology and Literature at the University of Chicago. His seminars and research explored the relations between poetry and religion, among other interdisciplinary concerns. His book of poems *A Sky of Late Summer* was published in 1963.

VITTORIA REPETTO, vice-president of the Italian American Writers' Association, has published widely in magazines and has hosted the long-running women's poetry program at Bluestockings Bookstore in New York City.

LOIS ROMA-DEELEY'S first book is *Rules of Hunger* (2004), her second, *NorthSight* (2006), and her third is *High Notes* (2010). She is the recipient of a Samuel T. Coleridge Literary Prize, and Poet in Residence at Paradise Valley Community College in Phoenix, Arizona.

JOE ROSS is the author of several books of poetry including *Strata* (2008). He has lived for extended periods of time in Washington, D.C. and San Diego and in both cities he was a vital part of the poetry community, organizing reading series among other arts activities. He presently resides in Paris.

CLARE ROSSINI'S most recent book is *Lingo* (2006). Her first book *Winter Morning With Crow* received the 1996 Akron Poetry Prize. She is on the faculties of Trinity College and the MFA in Creative Writing Program at Vermont College.

FRANK SAMPERI (1933-1991) published twenty books of poetry after having been discovered by Louis Zukofsky and Cid Corman. Samperi created a lifelong poem of pilgrimage through urban America and the world of the spirit. His selected poems, *Spiritual Necessity*, was published in 2004.

MARIA SASSI served recently as West Hartford, Connecticut's first poet laureate. She is a poet and playwright.

LESLIE SCALAPINO (1944-2010) was the groud-breaking, genre-stretching author of thirty books of poetry, poem-plays, essays, and fiction, including *way* (1998), which won the American Book Award, and *It's go in horizontal: Selected Poems 1974-2006* (2008).

JENNIFER SCAPPETTONE is the author of *From Dame Quickly* (2009) and of several chapbooks, including *Thing Ode / Ode oggenttuale* (2008), translated into Italian in converstion with Marco Giovenale. She teaches at the University of Chicago and she will be in residence at the American Academy in Rome as a Rome Prize Fellow in Modern Italian Studies in 2010-2011.

JOHN SKOYLES is the author of four books of poems, most recently, *The Situation* (2007). He teaches at Emerson College.

GILBERT SORRENTINO (1929-2006) is the author of more than thirty books of fiction, poetry, and criticism. He received a Lannan Literary Lifetime Achievement Award and taught at Stanford University for many years before returning to his native Brooklyn.

FELIX STEFANILE (1920-2009) started the poetry journal *Sparrow* in 1954 and for many years he taught at Purdue University. He published numerous books of poetry and translation, and received the John Ciardi Award for Lifetime Achievement in Poetry, among other distinctions.

JOHN TAGLIABUE (1923-2006), a member of the Bates College faculty from 1953 to 1989, authored six books of poetry including *New and Selected Poems, 1942-1997* (1998). He also had six Fulbright awards during his teaching career. This world traveler once called his poetry "on-the-spot, lyricism."

ALDO TAMBELLINI, writer, filmmaker, and multi-media artist, was a Fellow at the Center for Advanced Visual Studies at the Massachusetts Institute of Technology from 1976 to 1984. In 2007 he received the Lifetime Achievement Award from Syracuse University at the Syracuse International Film Festival.

THOM TAMMARO is Professor of English and Director of the MFA in Creative Writing Program at Minnesota State University. His collections of poems include *Holding on for Dear Life* (2004) and *When the Italians Came to My Home Town* (1995).

JOANNE TANGORRA'S poems have appeared in *Prairie Schooner, Indiana Review, Margie, The Antioch Review*, and other journals. She was awarded The Perillo Prize for Italian American writing.

MARIA TERRONE is the author of *The Bodies We Were Loaned* (2002) and *A Secret Room in Fall* (2006). In 2007 she received an Individual Artist Initiative Award from the Queens Council on the Arts. She is Assistant VP for Communications at Queens College.

JOSEPH TORRA is the author of numerous novels and books of poetry, including the Italian-American novel *They Say* (2007), and the autobiographical-fiction *Call Me Waiter* (2008).

CATHERINE TUFARIELLO'S book *Keeping My Name* received the 2006 Poets' Prize for the best book of verse published by an American in the preceding year. Her poems and translations from Italian have appeared in journals such as *The Hudson Review*, *Poetry*, and *Yale Italian Poetry*.

LEWIS TURCO, Professor Emeritus of English, was Founding Director of the Cleveland State University Poetry Center and the Program in Writing Arts at the State University of New York at Oswego. His classic *The Book of Forms: A Handbook of Poetics* has been continuously in print since 1968. His work has received a Choice "Outstanding Academic Book" award and the Melville Cane Award of the Poetry Society of America. For his poetry he has received the Bordighera Prize and the John Ciardi Award for Lifetime Achievement in Poetry.

JOSEPH TUSIANI emigrated from Italy to the United States in 1947 at the age of 23. In the U.S. he began his distinguished career as an educator, translator, and poet. In 1956 he was the first American to win the Greenwood Prize of the Poetry Society of England. Among Tusiani's many translations are *The Complete Poems of Michelangelo* (1960) and *Leopardi's canti* (1999). Among his works of poetry is *Ethnicity: Selected Poems* (2000). Tusiani is one of the most prolific Latin language poets of our age.

PAUL VANGELISTI has been an important figure at the intersection of contemporary American and Italian poetry. Ennio Corrente, the inspiration for the poem included herein, was a Communist party politician and city councilman from Modena. Vangelisti is the author of *Embarrassment of Survival: Selected Poems 1970-2000* (2001) and he directs the graduate writing program at Otis College of Art and Design in Los Angeles.

PASQUALE VERDICCHIO teaches at the University of California, San Diego. He has translated Antonio Gramsci's important work *The Southern Question* (2006), written on global culture in *Bound by Distance: Rethinking Nationalism through the Italian Diaspora* (1997), and published his poetry in *This Nothing's Place* (2008).

PAUL VOLI (1944-2011), is the author of twelve books, most recently *Overnight* (2007). He received the Zabel Award from the American Academy of Arts and Letters and the John Ciardi Lifetime Achievement Award in Poetry. He taught at Columbia University and the New School.

ROBERT VISCUSI received the American Book Award in 1996 for his novel *Astoria*. He is the author recently of the volume of poetry *A New Geography of Time* (2004) and the critical study *Buried Caesars, and Other Secrets of Italian American Writing* (2006). His current project is an epic poem entitled *Ellis Island.*

Permissions

Kim Addonizio: "Generations" from *Tell Me*. Copyright © 2000 by Kim Addonizio. Reprinted with permission of BOA Editions, Ltd., www.boaeditions.org.

Joe Amato: "Hotel" copyright © 2006 by Joe Amato, from *Under Virga*, published by Chax Press in 2006. Used by permission of Chax Press and the author.

Michael Anania: "Omaha Appendices: IV" from *Omaha Appendices*, published by Asphodel Books in 2010. Used by permission of Asphodel Books.

Christopher Arigo: "Archived imperatives I" copyright © 2007 by Christopher Arigo, from *In the archives*, published by Omnidawn in 2007. Used by permission of the author.

Anny Ballardini: "They came from the same place" copyright © 2010 by Anny Ballardini. Used by permission of the author.

J. T. Barbarese: "Our Fathers" copyright © 2005 by J. T. Barbarese, from *A Very Small World*, published by Orchises in 2005. Used by permission of the author.

Dennis Barone: "Map" copyright © 2011 by Dennis Barone, from *Parallel Lines*, published by Shearsman Books, Ltd. in 2011. Used by permission of the author.

Dorothy Barresi: "My Anger in 1934" copyright © 1996 by Dorothy Barresi, from *The Post-Rapture Diner*, published by the University of Pittsburgh Press in 1996. Used by permission of the author.

Joseph Bathanti: "Domenico Giusseppe" copyright © 2010 by Joseph Bathanti, from *Restoring Sacred Art*, published by Star Cloud Press in 2010. Used by permission of the author.

James Bertolino: "Distracted" copyright © 2009 by James Bertolino, from *Finding Water, Holding Stone*, published by Cherry Grove Collections in 2009. Used by ermission of the author.

Raymond L. Bianchi: selection from "American Master" copyright © 2006 by Raymond L. Bianchi, published by Moria Books in 2006. Used by permission of the author.

John Brandi: "Hymn for a Night Feast" copyright © 1988 by John Brandi, from *Hymn for a Night Feast*, published by Holy Cow Press in 1988. Used by permission of the author.

Stephen Campiglio: "Cause and Effect" copyright © 2010 by Stephen Campiglio. Originally published in *Italian Americana* in 2010. Used by permission of the author.

Mary Caponegro: "Introduction." Used by permission of the author.

Kara Candito: "Postcard: I've Been Meaning to Write –" copyright © 2009 Kara Candito, from *Taste of Cherry*, published by the University of Nebraska Press in 2009 (2008 Prairie Schooner Book Prize in Poetry). Used by permission of the author.

David Cappella: "The Clothespin" copyright © 2008 by David Cappella. Used by permission of the author.

Christine Casson: "Grace" copyright © 2008 by Christine Casson, from *After the First World*, published by Star Cloud Press in 2008. Used by permission of the author.

Grace Cavalieri: "Father" copyright © 1979 by Grace Cavalieri, from *Swan Research*, published by Word Works in 1979. Used by permission of the author.

Joseph Ceravolo: "The Green Lake Is Awake." *The Green Lake Is Awake: Selected Poems.* Coffee House Press, 1994. Used by permission of the Estate of Joseph Ceravolo, Rosemary Ceravolo, Executrix, and the publisher.

John Ciardi: "Back" from *Collected Poems of John Ciardi.* Copyright © 1997 by Edward Cifelli. Reproduced with the permission of the University of Arkansas Press.

David Citino: "Volare." *The Gift of Fire.* University of Arkansas Press 1986. *The Discipline, new and selected poems, 1980-1992.* Ohio State University Press, 1992. Used by permission of Mary Citino.

Ned Condini: "Saint Vincent Ferrer, New York" copyright © 2011 by Ned Condini. Used by permission of the author.

Gregory Corso: "Italian Extravaganza." *Gasoline.* City Lights Publishers, 1958 and 2001. Used by permission of the publisher.

Paola Corso: "The Doctor Makes His Diagnosis" copyright © 2004 by Paola Corso, from *Death by Renaissance*, published by Bottom Dog Press in 2004. Used by permission of the author.

Gerald Costanzo: "The White Experience in America" copyright © 1992 by Gerald Costanzo, from *Nobody Lives on Arthur Godfrey Boulevard*, published by BOA Editions in 1992. Used by permission of the author.

Peter Covino: "Wellington Diner Infidel" copyright © 2005 by Peter Covino, from *Cut Off the Ears of Winter*, published by New Issues in 2005. Used by permission of the author.

Pellegrino D'Acierno: "Warning" published in *Scattered Leaves*, Vigo Press, 1938. Used by permission of Pellegrino D'Acierno.

Rachel Guido deVries: "Italian Grocer" copyright © 1996 by Rachel Guido deVries, from *How to Sing to a Dago*, published by Guernica Editions in 1996. Used by permission of the author.

Diane di Prima: "Backyard" copyright © 1975 and 1989 by Diane di Prima. Used by permission of the author.

John Domini: "Lakeshore, L.A., Long Island, Ex-O-Skel." copyright © 2010. Used by permission of the author.

Elaine Equi: "Mulberry Street." *Ripple Effect: New and Selected Poems.* Coffee House Press, 2007. Used by permission of the author and the publisher.

Lawrence Ferlinghetti: "Autobiography" from *A Coney Island of the Mind*, copyright © 1958 by Lawrence Ferlinghetti. Reprinted by permission of New Directions Publishing Corp.

Vincent Ferrini: "Ellis Island Rediscovered" from *The Whole Song: Selected Poems*. Copyright © 2004 by Vincent Ferrini. Used with permission of the poet and the University of Illinois Press.

Diana Festa: "Afterwards" copyright © 2009 by Diana Festa, from *The Gathering*, published by Poetic Matrix Press in 2009. Used by permission of the author.

Jonathan Galassi: "Morning Run" copyright © 1998 by Jonathan Galassi, from *Morning Run*, published by Paris Review Editions in 1998. Used by permission of the author.

Mary Giaimo: "For Jessica, Between Continents" copyright © 2011 by Mary Giaimo. Used by permission of the author.

David Giannini: "Dusk" copyright © 2002 by David Giannini, from *Side-Ways*, published by Quale Press in 2002. Used by permission of the author.

Sandra Mortola Gilbert: "Mafioso" copyright © 1978 by Sandra Mortola Gilbert, from *In the Fourth World: Poems*, published by the University of Alabama Press in 1979. Used by permission of the author.

Maria Mazziotti Gillan: "Learning Grace" copyright © 2009 by Maria Mazziotti Gillan, from *What We Pass On: Collected Poems: 1980-2009*, published by Guernica Editions in 2010. Used by permission of the author.

Dana Gioia: "The Lost Garden" copyright © 2001 by Dana Gioia, from *Interrogations at Noon*, published by Graywolf Press in 2001. Used by permission of the author.

John Giorno: "La Saggezza Delle Streghe (Wisdom Of The Witches)" copyright © 2008 by John Giorno, from *Subduing Demons in America: Selected Poems 1962-2007*, published by Soft Skull Press in 2008. Used by permission of the author.

Daniela Gioseffi: "Orta Nova, *Provincia di Puglia*" copyright © 2007 by Daniela Gioseffi, from *Blood Autumn, Autunno di Sangue*, published by Bordighera Press in 2007. Used by permission of the author.

Peter Gizzi: "Wintry Mix" copyright © 2007 by Peter Gizzi, from *The Outernationale*, published by Wesleyan University Press in 2007. Used by permission of the author.

Rose Basile Green: "Fourteenth Sunday After Pentecost," *To Reason Why*. A. S. Barnes, 1971. Used by permission of Carol-Rae Green Sodano.

George Guida: "The Italian American Satan" copyright © 2006 by George Guida, from *Low Italian: Poems*, published by Bordighera Press in 2006. Used by permission of the author.

Gerry LaFemina: "Freight" copyright © 2001 by Gerry LaFemina, from *Zarathustra in Love*, published by Mayapple Press in 2001. Used by permission of the author.

Teresa Leo: "P.S." copyright © 2008 by Teresa Leo, from *The Halo Rule*, published by Elixir Press in 2008. Used by permission of the author.

P. H. Liotta: "The Blue Whale" copyright © 2007 by P. H. Liotta, from *The Graveyard of Fallen Monuments*, published by Quale Press in 2007. Used by permission of the author.

Gian Lombardo: "Field of View" copyright © 2004 by Gian Lombardo, from *Of All The Corners To Forget*, published by Meeting Eyes Bindery in 2004. Used by permission of the author.

Matthew Longabucco: "These My Exhortations" copyright © 2008 by Matthew Longabucco. Originally appeared on logolalia.com/arspoetica, December 30, 2008. Used by permission of the author.

Alessandra Lynch: "Carousel" copyright © 2008 by Alessandra Lynch, from *It was a terrible cloud at twilight*, published by Pleiades Press in 2008. Used by permission of the author.

Anne Marie Macari: "Annunciation" from *Gloryland.* Copyright © 2005 by Anne Marie Macari. Reprinted with the permission of Alice James Books, www.alicejamesbooks.org.

Gerard Malanga: "Giorgio Morandi" copyright © 2010 by Gerard Malanga, first published in *The Sienese Shredder* in 2010. Used by permission of the author.

Sarah Manguso: "Everything" copyright © 2006 by Sarah Manguso, from *Siste Viator,* published by Four Way Books in 2006. Used by permission of the author.

Mary Ann Mannino: "Leaf Leaving" copyright © 2008 by Mary Ann Mannino, first published in the *Paterson Literary Review* in 2008. Used by permission of the author.

Paul Mariani: "The Old Men Are Dying." *Crossing Cocytus.* Grove Press, 1982. Used by permission of the author.

Donna Masini: "Getting Out of Where We Came From" copyright © 1994 by Donna Masini, from *That Kind of Danger,* published by Beacon Press in 1994. Used by permission of Beacon Press.

Carole Maso: "You Were Dazzle" originally published by the Ecco Press in *Aureole* (1996) and reprinted by City Lights (2003). Used by permission of the author.

Stephen Massimilla: "Clairvoyante" copyright © 2001 by Stephen Massimilla. Originally published in *High Plains Literary Review* in 2001. Used by permission of the author.

Jerome Mazzaro: "Library Tapestry" copyright © 1966 and 2002 by Jerome Mazzaro. Used by permission of the author.

Albert Mobilio: "Pilgrims" copyright © 2002 by Albert Mobilio, from *Me with Animal Towering,* published by Black Square Editions in 2002. Used by permission of the author.

Stephen Murabito: "Ethnic Poem" copyright © 2006 by Stephen Murabito, from *Communion of Asiago,* published by Star Cloud Press in 2006. Used by permission of the author.

Michael Palma: "The Patron Saint of California" copyright © 2000 by Michael Palma, from *A Fortune in Gold*, published by Gradiva Publications in 2000. Used by permission of the author.

Michael Palmer: "Notes for Echo Lake 1" copyright © 1981 and 2001 Michael Palmer, from *Notes for Echo Lake*, published by North Point Press in 1981, and *Codes Appearing: Poems 1979-1988*, published by New Directions in 2001. Used by permission of the author.

Joseph Papaleo: "History Lesson for Friday." *Picasso at 91*. Seaport Poets & Writers Press, 1987. Reprinted by permission of Tonie Papaleo.

Jay Parini: "Grandmother in Heaven" copyright © 2005 by Jay Parini, from *The Art of Subtraction: New and Selected Poems*, published by George Braziller in 2005. Used by permission of the author.

Lucia Perillo: "Lament in Good Weather" copyright © 1999 by Lucia Perillo, from *The Oldest Map with the Name America*, published by Random House in 1999. Used by permission of the author.

Anthony Piccione: "Napping Outside" from *Seeing It Was So*. Copyright © 1986 by Anthony Piccione. Reprinted with the permission of BOA Editions, Ltd., www.boaeditions.org

Nick Piombino: "The Chase" copyright © 2003 by Nick Piombino. Originally published in *Sidereality* in 2003. Used by permission of the author.

Lia Purpura: "Though I Am Not." *Stone Sky Lifting*. The Ohio State University Press, 2000.

Henry Rago: "The Distances." *A Sky of Late Summer*. Macmillan, 1963. Used by permission of Christina Rago.

Vittoria Repetto: "La Bella Figura." *Not Just a Personal Ad*. Guernica Editions, 2006. Reprinted by permission of the author and the publisher.

Lois Roma-Deeley: "The Apostle of Wax and Shine" copyright © 2004 by Lois Roma-Deeley, from *Rules of Hunger*, published by Star Cloud Press in 2004. Used by permission of the author.

Joe Ross: selection from "An American Voyage" copyright © 1993 by Joe Ross, from *An American Voyage*, published by Sun & Moon Press in 1993. Used by permission of the author.

Clare Rossini: "The Diagrammer of Sentences" copyright © 2006 by Clare Rossini, from *Lingo*, published by the University of Akron Press in 2006. Used by permission of the author.

Frank Samperi: selection from "Anamnesis" from *Spiritual Necessity: Selected Poems of Frank Samperi*, edited by John Martone. Barrytown, NY: Station Hill Press, 2004. Used by permission of the publisher.

Maria Sassi: "Town Story" copyright © 1998 by Maria Sassi, from *Rooted in Stars*, published by Singular Speech Press in 1998. Used by permission of the author.

Leslie Scalapino: "wild gap of dawn – not it.." and "'seeing Venus in the morning sky..'", from *New Time* copyright © 1999 by Leslie Scalapino. Reprinted with permission of Wesleyan University Press and the estate of Leslie Scalapino.

Jennifer Scappettone: "An Abeyance" copyright © 2006 by Jennifer Scappettone, from *From Dame Quickly*, published by Litmus Press in 2009. Used by permission of the author.

John Skoyles: "Father Colombo." *A Little Faith*. Carnegie Mellon University Press, 1981. Used by permission of the author.

Gilbert Sorrentino: "The Memory." *New and Selected Poems: 1958-1998*. Green Integer, 2004. Used by permission of Christopher Sorrentino and the publisher.

Felix Stefanile: "The Americanization of the Immigrant." *The Country of Absence: Poems and an Essay*. Bordighera Press, 1999. Used by permission of Selma Stefanile and the publisher.

John Tagliabue: "Good Friday in Procida" published in *New and Selected Poems 1942-1997* by John Tagliabue 1997, National Poetry Foundation, University of Maine, Orono, ME. Used by permission of Grace Tagliabue.

Aldo Tambellini: "November 9, 1990" from www.aldotambellini.com. Used by permission of the author.

Thom Tammaro: "Richard M. Nixon: My Italian Problem" copyright © 2009 by Thom Tammaro. Originally published in *Italian Americana*, spring 2009 (online edition). Used by permission of the author.

Joanne Tangorra: "Photograph, 1920" copyright © 2002 by Joanne Tangorra. Originally published in the *South Dakota Review* in 2002. Used by permission of the author.

Maria Terrone: "Ghost Frescoes" copyright © 1999 by Maria Terrone. Originally published in *Poetry* in 1999. Used by permission of the author.

Joseph Torra: "Self-Portrait with a Loaf of Bread" copyright © 1996 by Joseph Torra, from *Keep Watching the Sky*, published by Zoland Books in 1996. Used by permission of the author.

Catherine Tufariello: "Keeping My Name" copyright © 2004 by Catherine Tufariello, from *Keeping My Name*, published by Texas Tech University Press in 2004. Used by permission of the author.

Lewis Turco: "An Immigrant Ballad" copyright © 2004 by Lewis Turco, from *Collected Lyrics of Lewis Turco / Wesli Court*, published by Star Cloud Press in 2004. Used by permission of the author.

Joseph Tusiani: "Song of the Bicentennial." *Gente Mia and Other Poems.* Italian Cultural Center, Stone Park, Illinois, 1978. Used by permission of the author.

Paul Vangelisti: "After Ennio Correnti, 1948-1997" copyright © 2007 by Paul Vangelisti, from *Days Shadows Pass*, published by Green Integer in 2007. Used by permission of the author.

Pasquale Verdicchio: "The Way Home" copyright © 2008 by Pasquale Verdicchio, from *This Nothing's Place*, published by Guernica Editions in 2008. Used by permission of the author.

Paul Violi : selection from "The Hazards of Imagery" copyright © 2000 by Paul Violi, from *Breakers: Selected Poems*, published by Coffee House Press in 2000. Used by permission of the author.

Robert Viscusi: "Picture of a Man with a Broken Heart" reprinted by permission of the author from *A New Geography of Time*. Guernica Editions, 2004.

Every effort has been made to obtain permission for all copyrighted poetry reprinted herein. If insufficient credit has been given to any copyright holder, please write to the editor in care of the publisher.

Index to Titles

CPSIA information can be obtained at www.ICGtesting.com
Printed in the USA
LVOW061150100911

245706LV00003B/1/P